The History of Roller Skating

**James Turner
In collaboration with
Michael Zaidman**

National Museum of Roller Skating
Lincoln, Nebraska

The History of Roller Skating
©1997 National Museum of Roller Skating
4730 South Street, P. O. Box 6579
Lincoln, Nebraska 68506
USA
e-mail: rllrsktmus@aol.com
http://www.usacrs.com/museum.htm

This book is fully protected by copyright and nothing that appears in it may be reprinted or reproduced in any manner, either wholly or in part, for any use whatsoever, without special permission of the copyright owner expressly permitting such reprint on each and every occasion. Printed and bound in the United States of America.

The National Museum of Roller Skating is a non-profit institution established in 1980. The museum exists as an autonomous entity to acquire, preserve, research, and interpret the history of roller skating through its collection of artifacts, photographs, archival materials, and other skating memorabilia. Its purpose is to sponsor and carry on activities and exhibits in order to educate both the general public and those associated with roller skating as a sport, business, and recreation.

The museum publishes the *Historical Roller Skating Overview*, a bi-monthly newsletter available to members, featuring historical articles and museum news. For further information about the museum and how to become a member, please write to the above address.

The cover of the book (clockwise from top left): Joe Laurey; Lauren Adams, Charlotte Vening and Kim Darnell; Joseph Jordan; Lowe's Roller Rink; Gloria Nord; Mecca rink sign; The Skaters Bijouve; 1941 Roller Skating Championship ticket; International Olympic Committee President, Juan Antonio Samaranch, from *Art I Esport A Catalunya* by Joan Bert I Padreny; 1885 Postcard; a Vaudeville roller skate; Shirley Snyder; Roller Hockey International players; "Funciones de Patines" (poster) by Jules Cheret.

The back cover (clockwise from top left): Skateland sticker; Saxe Signs hockey team; Gloria Nord and Doug Breniser.

ISBN 0-9658192-0-5

CONTENTS

Acknowledgments

Forward

1 *The Development of Skates, Early Origins*
2 *The Pioneers*
3 *The Evolution of Skates, 1863 to Present*
4 *The Boom Period, 1880-1910*
5 *Skating Associations*
6 *Origins of Skate Dances*
7 *The Origins of Figure & Free Skating*
8 *Pairs & Fours Skating*
9 *Speed*
10 *Roller Hockey*
11 *Stage & Show Skating*
12 *Skating Schools*
13 *Roller Skating Music*
14 *Artistic Skating Costumes*

Appendices
  Bibliography
  Name Index
  Subject Index
  Credits

ACKNOWLEDGEMENTS

First and foremost, we would like to express our appreciation to the many members of the National Museum of Roller Skating, without whom this publication would not have been possible. The contributions they have made, whether monetary or through the donation of historical artifacts and archival materials, have been vitally important in making the museum a success.

Our appreciation also goes to the Board of Trustees for their support: Bert Anselmi-President, Chester Fried-Vice-President, George Pickard-Secretary/Treasurer, Marvin Facher, G. B. Van Roekel, Katherine McDonell, Edmund Young, Robert Bollinger, Mills Lynn, Frank Cernik, Charlotte Groves, Charles Wahlig, and Trustee Emeritii James Turner, Michael Brooslin, and Scott Addison Wilhite.

Articles by Michael Brooslin, Chester Fried, and George Pickard have also been added to the text. The photography and other graphics were supplied by the National Museum of Roller Skating.

The museum wishes to thank the governing body of roller skating, USA Roller Skating (USARS) for providing the funding for this project and for their continued support of the museum. Also a sincere thank you to Jeanette Tupe, Publications Manager, for her effort towards making the graphics and layout of this book a success.

And special thanks to the many individuals who helped edit this book including: Sarah Davis, Dr. Janie Kyle, Christine Nienaber, Andy Seeley, and Jay Sorensen. Last but not least, we would like to acknowledge the research and editorial help of Assistant Curator Sarah Beth Mazo Webber.

FORWARD

Since this book was first published in 1975, roller skating has grown in popularity. In 1972, when my original research was done at the Library of Congress, there were only 30 books published on roller skating from 1872 to 1972. Since then there have been twice that many new books written about the sport of roller skating.

This second edition of *The History of Roller Skating* contains new information due to continued research, writing of magazine and newsletter articles, and new historical information not available in 1974.

The National Museum of Roller Skating began on October 27, 1980, when Bert Anselmi, Robert Bollinger, Marvin Facher, Chester Fried, George Pickard, Dick Young, and I signed the articles of incorporation to create the museum. The purpose of the new corporation: to obtain items of lasting interest or value related to roller skating; to care for and display these items in an institution open to the general public; to sponsor and carry on activities that foster a better understanding of the history and development of roller skating; to receive, invest, and manage gifts, grants, and bequests for any or all of these purposes.

The museum's current location is shared with the governing body of roller skating, USA Roller Skating. The museum occupies 2400 square feet of space, including an exhibits floor, Director/Curator's office, Library/Archives room, and storage space. The Archives room contains approximately 1500 volumes of historical information, over 8,000 photographs, scrapbooks of individuals prominent in roller skating from 1900 to the present, archives dealing with competitive roller skating events dating back to the 1800's, and over 100 American and foreign periodicals.

James Turner 1997

1 THE DEVELOPMENT OF SKATES
Early Origins

The idea of easy personal movement has been with us for centuries. Man has tried to invent many methods of personal transportation. The word "skate" can be traced back to an early definition meaning to "shoot ahead or slide." In Old English it was spelled "scate," in Italian "scatta," and in Dutch "schoats."

In early history, no evidence exists of skating in southern cultures. Neither the Greek nor the Roman languages refer to skates or skating. However, in northern countries (modern England, Scandinavia, and the Netherlands), the people developed skating as a form of winter transportation when iced over waterways were convenient and roads were blocked by snow. The Finns were called "Skird Finnai," the sliding Finns, because of their famous skates (strips of wood, turned up in the front, tied to the feet of the user). Wood and bone runners were first used for skate blades and artifacts of these have been found in Holland, Sweden, Iceland, and England dating from 1100 A.D. The skating technique has been described as follows, "binding under their feet the shin bones of some animal and taking in their hands, poles shod with iron which they strike at times against the ice, they are carried along with as great rapidity as a bird flying."

References about skating occur in old Runic poetry, Norse mythology, and in the "Edda," a collection of Icelandic poems written in the 1200s. Skating was a fully recognized sport and athletic skill at least around the age of the Crusades, some 700 years ago. Keep in mind this was ice skating. What about wheels? Unfortunately, the inventor of the first roller skate is not known for sure. Evidence asserts that in Holland, where the Dutch avidly skated on ice, one enthusiast could not bear the spring and summer off skates. He produced a wheeled skate with several wooden spools in a line to simulate ice skating on pavement. Thus, the roller skate was born out of the desires of a frustrated ice skater. The Dutchman, Hans Brinker, may have been this first roller skater.

John Joseph Merlin

1743 marks the first recorded use of roller skates on the stage of the Old Drury Lane Theatre in London, England, during the performance of a play by Tom Hood. The first recorded man to invent a roller skate was John Joseph Merlin. Born in the city of Huys, Belgium, on September 17, 1735, Merlin became a maker of musical instruments and a general mechanical tinkerer. He moved to London in 1760 because he was invited by the Royal Academy of Science to work for them. He lived on Soho Square with the Ambassador of Spain, Count de Fuentes. He became the director of the Cos Museum, and there displayed many of his inventions including a piano, an organ, and a combination piano-harpsichord. Merlin exhibited at other museums too - one on Princes Street and another on Oxford Street, which became known as "Merlin's Cave." Among his clever mechanical inventions, Merlin created a pair of skates with small metal wheels. One evening he was invited to a party at Mrs. Corneily's on Soho Square. It was a masquerade at Carlisle-House, a big estate in London. As his costume, he donned his roller skates and a violin and began to skate around the party playing the instrument. Although well known as an inventor and musician, Joseph Merlin was not a very good skater. He could not control his speed or command his skates to go in the desired direction, and wildly crashed landed into a huge and expensive mirror (500 £ value), smashed it to bits, severely wounded himself, broke his violin, and set roller skating technique back to the drawing boards.

After Merlin's disaster, nothing more was heard of roller skating for thirty years until in 1790, Maximillian Lodewijk Van Lede, from Paris, made a Patin-A-Terre, which means a "ground skate." Monsieur Van Lede was in Paris to study painting and sculpture. The climate there bothered him and he went back to his hometown of Bruges. He had a reputation for eccentric behavior. He enjoyed ice skating and one might suppose that he invented his roller skate to use in a more temperate climate. Also in 1790, there is an engraving of a Swiss skater using what is probably Van Lede's skates. The invention became known in Germany as the "Erdschlittschuh." This skate was mentioned in the "Almanac de Gotha," a book of useful and new inventions.

Almanac de Gotha

Roller skates made it into the ballet entitled "The Artist of Winter Pleasures" in Berlin (1818). It was impossible at that time to successfully make ice for stage productions so actors used roller skates to simulate the ice skating scenes.

In the following year, 1819, roller skaters appeared on the streets of Paris and that same year the french government granted Monsieur Petitbled a patent on a roller skate, the first patent ever taken out on a roller skate. Petitbled claimed that anyone could use his skates to do the same things that could be done on ice skates. The design was a sole of wood with several rollers arranged in a straight line, the wheels were made of either wood, metal, or "deluxe" ivory. Each roller was the same size and only straight forward skating was attempted. Even turning a corner was a major physical feat and edges (a curve) and turns were almost impossible. Petitbled's skate was not all he claimed it to be.

The first patented in-line roller skate, 1819

Along the same line as the Petitbled skate was the "Volito," patented in 1823 by Robert John Tyers of Picadilly, London, England. Described as an "apparatus to be attached to boots, shoes, and other covering for the feet, for the purpose of traveling for pleasure," the Volito had five wheels in a line. Unlike the Petitbled skate, Tyers wheels were made of unequal size, with the center wheel larger. Tyers claimed that this made it possible to curve by shifting the body weight either forward or backward and roll on two wheels. Because of the unequal diameter of the wheels, the skate turned, with the skater never on more than two wheels at a time. The Volito also had a braking device, a hook that dragged at either the front or back to assist in stopping. This may be the first use of toe stops on a roller skate. The Tyers skate was used in an exhibition of roller skating given on a tennis court on Windmill Street, Haymarket, London, but it still did not catch the public fancy, with no great increase of skaters evident.

Tyers' Volito Skate

8

A watchmaker from Vienna named Lohner patented a skate in 1825. The Austrian government granted him a patent for a "mechanical wheeled skate." Lohner made his skate with a wooden sole and three brass wheels, one in front and two in back, like a tricycle. One new feature of this skate was the ratchet device designed to prevent the skater from rolling backwards. Several other inventors patented these forward only skates at a later date in the United States. Evidently, such skates were not for fancy or backward skating. Also in 1825, the ballet master Robillon used roller skates to simulate an ice skating scene in his production "The Alpine Dairy Maid," in Bordeaux, France.

A skate made by Jean Garcin appeared in France in 1828. It was very similar to the Volito skate, with three wheels in a line, the largest being in the center. Garcin also wrote about skating in his book, "Le Vrai Patineur" (The True Skater) he outlined 31 figures to practice. He built a large gymnasium, opened a roller rink there, held classes, and encouraged ice skaters to switch to rollers in warm weather. Unfortunately, his skate, called a "Cingar," an anagram of his own name, was not easy to use. There were no actions on the straight alignment of the wheels and skating edges or curves were nearly impossible. Garcin had to close his rink after a short time due to many accidents caused by the skates.

During the 1830s, roller skates were used occasionally for stage productions and some outdoor exhibitions, but there was no widespread use. Skaters existed as novelties used to attract attention to oneself, much like a unicycle seen on the street today compared to the more common bicycles.

Cingar Patented Roller Skate, 1828

Two ever popular side attractions--pretty women and beer--fostered the popularity of roller skating in Germany in the 1840s. A tavern in Berlin, the Corso Halle, featured pretty female waitresses on roller skates. A contemporary newspaper article described the action: "The moment a customer takes his seat, one of the damsels darts from the end of the room, skims over the floor, describes clever curves round the end of a table or a cluster of chairs, brings herself up at the moment he thinks it is inevitable she must glide over his toes--and requests to know his wishes. She often collects several orders in the course of a round or from a single group; and will skate back with any number of pint pots of beer in both hands; without disturbing a single flake of froth. Except from the rattling noise produced, the motion is as good an imitation of ice skating as can be conceived. To the curious stranger, no secret is made of the mechanisms employed. Small iron wheels, let into the sole of a strong, but neatly fitting pair of boots, are all the mystery. But to move about in them easily, and even gracefully, requires much practice. It is also more fatiguing than walking, and towards midnight, when it may be assumed each waitress had skated several miles, they all look rather weary."

The "Grand Opera" in 1849 put roller skating into the highest art form. Giacomo Meyerbeer, the great German composer, wrote two grand operas, "Robert le Diable" (1831) and "Les Hugenots" (1836). These quite successful operas established his fame after they became part of the operatic repertoire. For his next opera, Meyerbeer took a plot from history, the religious revolt in the 1530s by Westphalian Anabaptists led by the revolutionary John Bockholt. Meyerbeer based his opera on actual historical events, but went along with the common practice of his day and took many liberties with the facts. His male lead singer was not the best, so Meyerbeer began developing another character in the plot to feature the outstanding voice of a female contralto, Pauline Viardot-Garcia. At this time a French inventor, Louis Legrand, invented a roller skate. Meyerbeer, though an excellent composer, was a genius at stage production. After seeing a demonstration of these roller skates, he designed an entire scene, an Anabaptist Ice Carnival, to feature the new invention. Legrand made skates for the entire corps de ballet and gave lessons on their use. There were two models of this skate Legrand created. The men's skate with a wooden plate and two wheels, one placed at each end. The ladies model had four wheels with coupled pairs at each end of the plate, much like modern roller skates. Because of the beautiful voice of Viardot-Garcia and wonderful effect of a winter scene, complete with simulated ice skaters, the opera "Le Prophete" was a huge success. Meyerbeer took Le Prophete on the road to several major cities including London. Legrand obtained a patent for his "Prophete Skate" on August 21, 1849. Sold in Paris, increasing numbers of skaters used Legrand's skates on paved streets, marble, and parquet floors. The publicity for roller skating was immense and skating on wheels became a fad in many European cities.

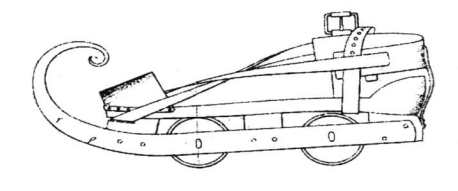

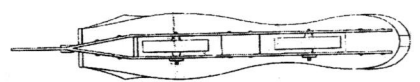

Legrand Skate

At about the same time as Meyerbeer's Le Prophete, the ballet composer and choreographer Paul Taglioni, known for incorporating new inventions and novel ideas in his productions, wrote a new ballet, "Les Plaisirs de l'Hiver ou Les Patineurs" (The Pleasures of Winter or The Skaters). Included in this ballet was a winter sports scene with roller skates used to imitate ice skating. Taglioni masked the wheels to represent ice skates and covered the floor with a smooth material to look like the frozen Danube River. The scenery, costumes, and music drew applause but the roller skaters created a sensation, "filling the audience with delight and surprise, and kept up constant laughter and applause."

These two operas gave roller skating something it did not have before: widespread popular appeal. All over Europe in the 1850s people started roller skating. The skates used were four iron wheels attached "in-line" to a wooden plate. In 1857 the old Cingar skate made another appearance at the Worlds Fair in Paris and roller skaters gave demonstrations.

In 1859, a new skate was developed in London called the Woodward skate, which featured wheels made from vulcanized India rubber. The skate had four wheels, one at each end and a coupled pair in the middle, with middle wheels slightly larger than the end wheels. The rubber wheels did not slip as much as wood or metal wheels. American skater and ballet master Jackson Haines used the skate to perform exhibitions in Europe in the 1860's. In 1864 Haines skated at Alhambra Theater (London) and later in "Le Prophete."

The first two successful rinks opened in 1876 in Paris and Berlin. A year later, the "Rollodrome" in Frankfort and "The Skating Palace" in Paris opened. The largest rink in Europe opened in London, called the "Grand Hall Olympia" with 68,000 square feet. The skating surface was as big as a football field. Originally opening in 1890, the Grand Hall Olympics soon closed, though it re-opened from 1909-1912 when the World Speed Championships were held in London.

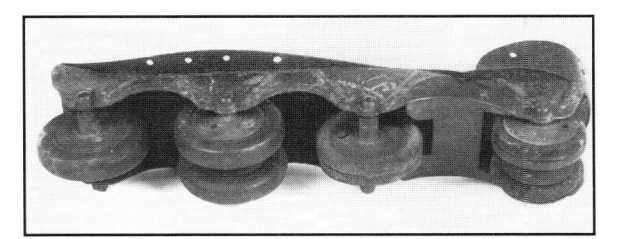

Woodward Skate

2 THE PIONEERS

James L. Plimpton

It was not until 1863 that the four wheeled turning roller skate was invented. In January of that year, James L. Plimpton of New York City patented his new invention. The mechanism had a pivoting action dampened by a rubber cushion which permitted the roller skate to curve, simply by leaning weight in the desired direction of travel. A similar patent was taken out in England in 1865. At last a roller skater could move around the floor as if he were on ice. One foot and two foot turns could be done easily and momentum could be built up by an out and in scissors movement, a difficult feat to do on former skate models.

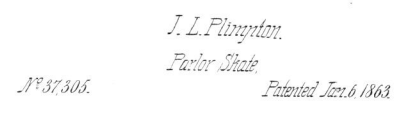

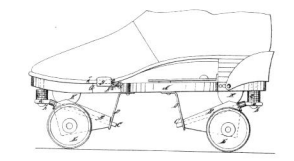

Plimpton was in the furniture business in New York City at this time, and he built a roller skating floor in his offices. He leased out skates rather than selling them, as he was promoting skating to the clergy and city officials as a supervised sport for young ladies and gentlemen--not for the masses. He founded the NYRSA (New York Roller Skating Association) to promote the sport of roller skating.

His original 1863 model had solid triangular shaped pieces on the truck assembly with round rubber cushions placed between the triangles. A wooden plate and a pivot rod allowed the wheels to turn. There were adjustable toe and heel clamps to fasten the skate to the shoe.

The later "improved" model dates from 1866. Evidently the toe clamps did not work well and leather buckle straps were added to the heel and toe. The placement of the rubber action pads changed from directly under the plate to two pieces on the sides of the truck assembly. The distinctive metal side braces were also added to the wheels. This is the Plimpton skate that became popular world wide.

1863 Plimpton Roller Skate

In the summer of 1866, the NYRSA leased the Atlantic House, a fashionable resort hotel in Newport, Rhode Island, and converted the dining room into a skating area. Suites were leased to NYRSA members and their guests. This was the first roller skating rink open to the public in the United States.

Newport officials, upper class New Englanders, and International celebrities were frequent visitors of the Atlantic House Skating Resort. Through his international contacts at Atlantic House, Plimpton began promoting his skating program world wide. His early proficiency test medal had the seals of twenty different countries where Plimpton skates were in use by 1870.

The invention of the Plimpton action skate quickly revolutionized the roller skate

Atlantic House

THE PLYMPTON SKATE.

The Plympton Skate is too well known to need any extended description, having been used in rinks for nearly twenty years. We are now prepared to offer this skate to the trade and to rinks at a price corresponding with other skates on the market.

Sizes from 7 1-2 to 11 1-2.   Price, per pair, $3.00.

Price List of Parts.

Ebonized Foot Boards	per pair, $0 40
Heel Straps	35
Toe "	25
Heel Bands	each 7
Trucks	" 20
Hangers	" 20
Steel Axles	" 10
Turkey Boxwood Wheels	" 5
Cotters	per 100, 35
Large Screws	each, 3
Rubbers	per doz., 35
Double Rivet Buckles	per gross, 1 50

Infringer Advertisement

PLIMPTON'S ROLLER SKATE
As advertised in *Spalding's Manual of Roller Skating*, 1884

The principle of Plimpton's skate as illustrated in *The Champion Skate Book*, c. 1879

industry. Although Plimpton became wealthy from his invention, there were so many infringements on his patents (as many as three hundred), that his lawyers made up form letters to warn offenders.

His son Henry Richardson Plimpton was also a skate inventor. Plimpton invented a cone and ball bearing wheel made from a red plastic substance.

In 1876 the famous English novelist, Charles Dickens, then a reporter for the London newspapers, wrote a story on roller skating. He credits Plimpton with inventing the wood skating floor; "narrow strips of wood, so sawn from the timber and placed on the floor that the grain of the wood in none of the strips is parallel to the surface of the floor." Dickens described the Plimpton skate as the "rocking skate;" others called it the "circular gliding skate."

During the 1870s, Plimpton himself toured rinks giving classes in basic skating techniques. A typical class series ran for one week, with one afternoon and one evening class each day. The full series of five classes cost $2.00 including skate rental, though Plimpton taught the afternoon classes for half price. These were the first group roller skating classes taught in America. The Plimpton Skate Company also opened rinks in the New England states.

In 1875, Plimpton visited England and testified in court about his role in the process of the development of roller skates. He stated, "I have been interested or engaged more or less for the past thirty years, in mechanical pursuits and I consider that during that period I have acquired a fair theoretical and practical knowledge of mechanics. About the year 1861, being in bad health, I was advised to practice ice skating and I derived much benefit from it; and when I could not practice upon the ice, I resorted to roller skating and I purchased a pair of roller skates of the most improved construction on sale in New York. I found it almost impossible to force the skate to the right or the left. From the time of ascertaining this, which happened about the month of March, 1862, to the middle of September or October in the same year, I made various experiments; and step by step I succeeded in making a roller skate which I could control in curves by moving the axis of the rollers out of parallel by rocking the footstock laterally." And thus the origin of the Plimpton roller skate.

After over 100 years of advancement, the Plimpton action skate, wood skating floors, class lessons, and proficiency tests all testify to one of history's greatest skating innovators, James Leonard Plimpton. Many artifacts of the Plimpton era are on display at the National Museum of Roller

Skating including the patent model of his skate that revolutionized the sport.

In 1865 Jackson Haines, an American ballet master and ice skating champion, took the European skating scene by storm. His dashing style and ballet movements became the basis of modern International Style figure and freestyle skating. His students were the leaders in developing figure skating and organizing the first world competitions in the 1880s on ice. Haines was also a good roller skater and liked to do both roller and ice skating. He was a star on roller skates in an imitation winter scene from the opera, "Le Prophete" by Meyerbeer.

In the early 1860s, Haines invented a new kind of ice skate. This solid and reliable skate allowed Jackson to develop his free skating ideas without fear of the usual mechanical failures. His skate served as the model for ice skates for the next 70 years. Haines was able to perfect a "sitting spin" which still bears his name. The Jackson Haines Spin took nine years to develop before he was satisfied with its execution. Haines was named U.S. Figure skating champion (ice) in 1863.

During the Civil War, his business as a ballet master and entertainer was almost at a standstill. Haines decided to leave the U.S. and seek a better life in Europe. In 1864 he went to England and gave a number of skating exhibitions. His new style of ballet-skating did not impress the Victorian skaters, who like many Americans remained satisfied to inscribe fancy figures in a formal atmosphere.

Next Haines traveled to Stockholm, where he began a skating tour of the capitols of Europe. Everywhere he skated he gained admiration, but he was best received in Vienna. Perhaps his ballet moves were really appreciated in this music and dancing capitol. He taught the population the waltz on skates and started a skate dancing craze in 1865.

JACKSON HAINES

The greatest original skater that ever lived. He was born and brought up near Troy, NY. He became prominent in skating circles in 1863, and during the winter of 1863-4 he gave skating exhibitions throughout the United States and Canada.

Jackson Haines was so influential that the "Vienna School of Skating" was founded, which evolved into the system known as International Style. The British school was in favor of controlled figure skating, but the Viennese school accepted expressive freestyle skating as a part of the total skater. Haines often used an orchestra to add musical accompaniment to his performances.

For several years, Jackson toured Europe skating on both roller and ice skates. He usually skated solo acts, except once when dressed as a polar bear he skated with one of his students, Franz Belazzi. Haines played the trained bear doing skating tricks and Belazzi played the animal trainer in the act.

Using a variety of costumes, good musical interpretation, and ballet

> 1863-1908
> FIRST DEMONSTRATION
> IN U.S.A. OF
> **FIGURE SKATING**
> in the
> INTERNATIONAL STYLE
> Braeburn Country Club
> Cambridge Skating Club
> Country Club of Brookline
> FEB 22ND 1908
> by
> IRVING BROKAW
> CHAMPION OF AMERICA 1906
> St. Nicholas Skating Club
> KARL ZENGER
> CHAMPION OF GERMANY 1906
> Munich Skating Club
> J. F. BACON
> CHAMPION OF AMERICA 1893
> Cambridge Skating Club
> in the
> AMERICAN STYLE
> First carried to Europe
> by
> JACKSON HAINES
> in 1864

movements performed on skates, Jackson Haines was a real showman and an international star. He played all the courts of Europe and even became considered a close friend of Czar Alexander II of Russia. People built rinks his honor and christened children for him. In 1882 at the first World Figure Skating Championship the prize was a statuette in the likeness of Jackson Haines. Appropriately, a student of Haines' won the competition, Leopold Frey.

In the Spring of 1875, after 11 years of exhibitions, Haines prepared to return to America. Caught in a blizzard while traveling between St. Petersburg and Stockholm, Haines contracted pneumonia and died in the small town of Gama-Karleby, Finland. His tombstone said it all: "Jackson Haines - American Skating King."

Jackson Haines left a fantastic legacy! He almost single-handedly revolutionized skating and popularized it. His conception of combining ballet and gymnastic tricks while skating to music is the foundation of modern freestyle skating. In addition to being the first professional show skater he invented the modern ice figure skate, the sit spin, and founded the International Style. As one of the original dance skaters he advocated roller skating. He believed that a good skater could do both ice and roller skating equally well, and he proved it!

Jackson Haines gives an exhibition in the St. Petersburg arena in Russia, 1865

Jackson Haines

3 THE EVOLUTION OF SKATES
1863 to Present

LEVANT M. RICHARDSON

Everett Hosmer Barney of the Barney and Berry Skate Co., Springfield, Massachusetts, marketed the first all metal skate in 1864. This company made ice and roller skates, and on some models the wheels and blades interchanged. Barney also invented the metal screw clamp to hold the skates to the shoe in 1866. Most skates of this era were fastened on with leather straps and buckles.

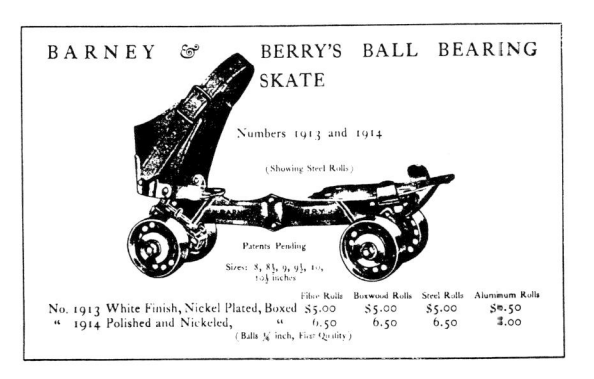

There were many patents on skates in the 1870s, but most were either not successful or infringements on Plimpton patents. The Samual Winslow Roller Skate Co., founded in 1857, manufactured ice and later roller skates. In 1880, Samual Winslow introduced the "Vineyard Model" roller skate which became the most popular skate of the 1880 boom period. By 1886, Winslow produced 260,000 pairs of skates annually; 40 ice and 15 roller models. Under the leadership of Winslow's son, Samual E. Winslow, the company continued to develop until 1930. It was the largest seller of skates in the world, over one million pairs a year. Many noted the Winslow skate had a good action, with boxwood or maple wheels, a durable plate, and an oiling system via a hollowed out axle.

The Henley Roller Skate became another popular skate in the 1880's. Micajah C. Henley of Richmond, Indiana received a patent in 1881 for his skate. The main improvement of the Henley skate was to make the tension on the skate cushions adjustable by means of a screw, much like the modern "kingbolt." This enabled the skater to adjust the performance of the skate to suit oneself. Henley skates were made until about 1915. The hump back curve shape of the plate is easily recognizable. The National Museum of Roller Skating incorporated the Henley Skate into its logo because of its unique shape.

Henley Roller Skate

Walter Ware invented a roller skate and tried to interest a Chicago sports promoter, Paddy Harmon (the builder of Chicago Stadium) to use this skate in a rink promotion. Harmon took one look at the early model skate and contemptuously threw it back at Ware, telling him the skate was no good. Ware took his skate, worked on it some more, and developed the basic Chicago Roller Skate in 1905. The company's business mushroomed and orders flooded in. The shop expanded from a small loft into a large factory in Chicago that turned out hundreds of models. In the 1930s, Chicago skates overtook Winslow as the leading skate in America.

In the 1930s, a big discussion occurred over which wheel pivot angle was the best, 45 or 10 degrees. Chicago Skate made several models of both angles throughout the 1940's. A 10 degree action gave firmer edges while a 45 degree action gave a quicker turning response. By the 1950s, the 10 degree was used for general skating and dance and 45 degree mostly for speed skates.

The Snyder Skate developed by Charles Snyder in the 1940s, introduced double action trucks. Many believed the double action trucks gave the skater more control, especially in figures, since the rubber cushions on the top and bottom of the truck assembly could flex with the skaters shift in weight to make firmer edges. The Snyder Skate also introduced the adjustable pivot pin which allowed fine tuning of the action. With every turn of the king bolt, the pivot pin sat into the socket of the hanger, giving the best skating response.

Skates of the Plimpton era (1860s) had no ball bearings to assist the wheels in rolling. The wheels fit right over the axles and were lubricated with oil. Most skaters carried a small oil can to use in the frequent oiling. The Winslow skate had a hollow axle and a oil reservoir to get the oil to the inside of the wheel.

James Plimpton's son, Henry Richardson Plimpton, patented a ball bearing system he called the "silent wheel." It had three sets of balls inside the wheel. However, Levant M. Richardson invented the most popular ball bearing system. He operated a roller rink in Milwaukee, Wisconsin in the Exposition Building in 1881. The skates used at the time were plain bearing "Muncie" skates manufactured by Thaddeus Neely of Muncie, Indiana. Richardson left Milwaukee and operated rinks in Janesville, Wisconsin and Freeport, Illinois. During this time he came up with the idea to use steel ball bearings in roller skate wheels which evolved into the modern system to facilitate better and have a smoother roll. He received a patent in 1884. The use of the ball bearing was a revolutionary development for roller skaters. Less friction meant easier and faster rolling wheels. Skating was now a less strenuous activity, resulting in a greater popularity of the sport. Mr. and Mrs. Richardson, both accomplished skaters, often did fancy skating exhibitions in Chicago at the Casino Rink and other rinks he managed. In 1898 Levant started the Richardson Ball Bearing and Skate Company. Most professional racers of the era used Richardson skates including Harley Davidson, Fred Martin, and Jesse Carey. Richardson even marketed a line of Harley Davidson Skating Boots in 1915. As an inventor, manufacturer, rink operator, and skating promoter, Levant M. Richardson is one of the fathers of the modern roller skating business.

Jimmy and Joan Lidstone introduced precision bearings to America in 1938. They used Polar Skates from Germany and "radial" type precision bearings from electric motors. These are made to accept the skater's weight straight downward and maintain a silent and even roll. Figure and dance skaters changed to precision immediately, but the speed skaters stayed with loose ball bearings until the 1970s when most speed competitors went to precision bearings.

The materials used for roller skate wheels changed greatly over the years. In the Plimpton era, wheels were made from the hard, fine grained, dense wood taken from the Boxwood or Flowering Dogwood tree that became the most popular, although metal and rubber were also used. Manufacturers also used the wood to make engravers blocks, musical, and mathematical instruments like slide rules. By 1900, most used maple wood for wheels. Rink managers sprinkled rosin powder on the floor to give more traction to

Snyder's double-action trucks

PERFECTION IS THE .. RESULT OF EXPERIENCE.

Do not be deceived by imitators who tell you they can furnish Skates "just as good." Dont assume the risk of buying Skates without reputation.

**—— THE ——
RICHARDSON**

Cushion Frame, Anti-Jar, Ball-Bearing Skates are

THE BEST IN THE WORLD.

wooden wheels on a wood floor.

In the 1940s the Chicago Skate Company made solid steel wheels, hollow steel, aluminum alloy, fibre composition wheels, five models of maple wood wheels, hard rubber, and soft rubber wheels. Steel wheels were for outdoor, fibre composition for rentals and hockey, and aluminum alloy for shows and speed. Chicago Skate made wood wheels for dance, figure skating, and speed.

In the 1930s, John L. Wintz created quality plastic lipstick cases and cigarette lighters in California. A skating friend asked Wintz to make some plastic skate wheels. Wintz said he'd try and in 1935, he designed wheels of clear Lucite. This wheel evoked interest among California rink operators. Wintz began experimenting with fiber and rubber combinations and developed a wheel of hard fiber and rubber inlays to prevent slipping. The Sure-Grip wheel was born. Due to the war, however, production remained limited until 1946. Today, Sure-Grip is a leading manufacturer of skates and wheels.

Vernon Fowlkes founded another major wheel company in 1949. Fowlkes worked for a company that made rubber belts. He used some of this material to develop a rubber-plastic skate wheel, called the Fomac Wheel. The Raybestos-Manhatten Co., which is famous for brake linings, also marketed a skate wheel in 1950, that became very popular.

Fomac, Sure-Grip, and Raybestos companies were the basis of most wheels of the 1950s and 1960s. In 1965, designers developed new polyurethane plastic compounds and used them for wheels, a spin-off from space age technology as the material was first used to seal space vehicles. These wheels gave better traction and roll. In the 1970s, a boom in outdoor skating began and polyurethane wheels marketed by Metaflex, 8 Red Wheels of Canada, and several skateboard companies, including Powell-Bones, became popular. These were most popular on concrete and plastic coated surfaces where the wheels needed extra traction.

The floor at the United States Amateur Confederation of Roller Skating's (USAC/RS) National Championships changed from sanded wood to a plastic coated maple floor in the 1970s. This did not change the wheels then in use since many rinks with plastic coated floors held the regional meets. Perry Giles, of Muskegon, Michigan, pioneered plastic floor coating many years before; however, speed skaters found that traditional wooden speed wheels did not work as well on the plastic coated floor, especially after the banning of rosin powder. Rink owners soon found that over sized skateboard wheels worked very well on plastic coated floors. The speed skaters took this idea and discovered good results with the larger diameter, softer wheels.

The Vanguard Company, headed by former champion John Matejec, developed several new urethane wheels, notably the Hugger for speed and Tiger Claws for artistic skating. Powell-Bones Corporation in California adapted their skateboard wheels for use on roller skates. In the early 1990's former World Speed Champion Tom Peterson developed the Hyper Wheel, and remains very popular in both artistic and speed skating.

Toe stops have been on skates since the earliest models. Most of these devices were for stopping, boot protection, balancing, or freestyle use. People considered early toe stops novelties and they did not generally catch on. The first documented toe stop was part of a parlour skate patented by Cyrus W. Saladee on May 16, 1876. The toe stop was called a "pad" and there was one on the front and rear of the Saladee Skate. Dominicus Brix in 1884 invented the adjustable stop. Two years later in 1886, J.A. Yarger invented a skate with "brakes." The screw in the slot allowed one to adjust the length of the toe stop on the front of the skate. In 1908, John Hohenadel of Philadelphia patented a skate with a rubber cushion attached to the front of the plate, similar to the modern design toe stops.

In the 1930's, most commercial skates did not have toe stops. With the introduction of International Style in 1938, the freestyle skaters became interested in toe stops to assist them on jumps and toe movements. At first skaters tried "shoe shop specials," pieces of rubber, or shoe heels, glued or nailed to the toe of the boot. However, skaters did not find such modifications satisfactory, and rink owners constantly complained that the nails used often scarred the wood floors at the rink. The freestylists wanted a more substantial jump stop to use like an ice skater's toe pick. Early freestyle skaters executed toe jumps like the mapes, flip, and lutz by tapping the toe of the boot or the side of a wheel on the take off. Only the most expert skater could do this. In 1939, National Champion Walter Stakosa performed a single mapes and a single flip without toe stops in his winning routine.

Freestyle skaters saw the toe stop as a way for roller skaters to jump like an ice skater. The number of "do-it-yourself" devices increased and so did the rink owners opposition. The controversy came to a head in 1947, when the Roller Skating Rink Operators Association ruled that toe stops would not be allowed in that year's competitions. This action resulted in a storm of protest by skaters and coaches. By December of that year the Board of Directors reconsidered and rescinded the ban on toe stops.

Noted skater and teacher Earl Van Horn, invented a "Jump-Spin-Stop" in 1945 that bolted onto the front truck and axle assembly. The Brook's Shoe Company put a threaded metal sleeve on the toe of their boot so that a toe stop could be screwed into it. In the late 1940s, the Rosco Toe Jumper became a popular "bolt on" toe stop assembly. However, the rubber only had a 3/16" bolt that frequently came loose or broke off.

Eli Fackler, a Swiss born engineer, living in Detroit, Michigan, with a background in skiing and ice skating developed the modern 5/8" threaded toe stop. An amateur coach for top senior ladies competitor Delores Molla, Fackler invented a succession of various jump stops for her to use. Fackler's early model consisted of a horseshoe shaped plate that bolted around the Snyder hanger, the toe stop a round rubber cap molded on a 5/8" aluminum bolt. The hanger had a set screw to make the toe stop adjustable in height and keep it tight while jumping. In 1947, Fackler began casting the toe stop fixture into a plate as is done today. The Snyder Skate company bought his design in the 1950s and "The Eli" toe stop design became the industry standard.

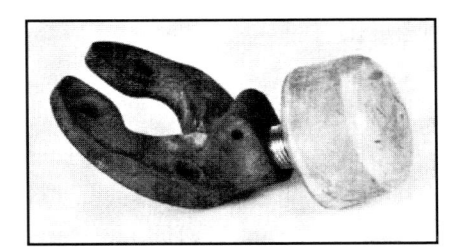

Fackler's Toe Stop

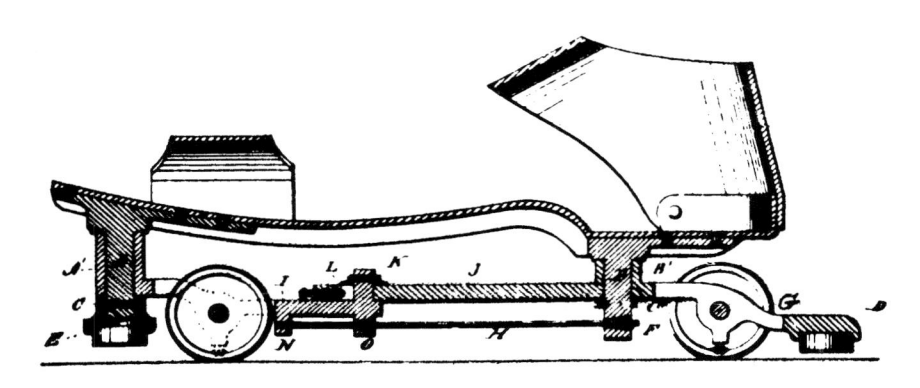

Saladee Roller Skate, 1876

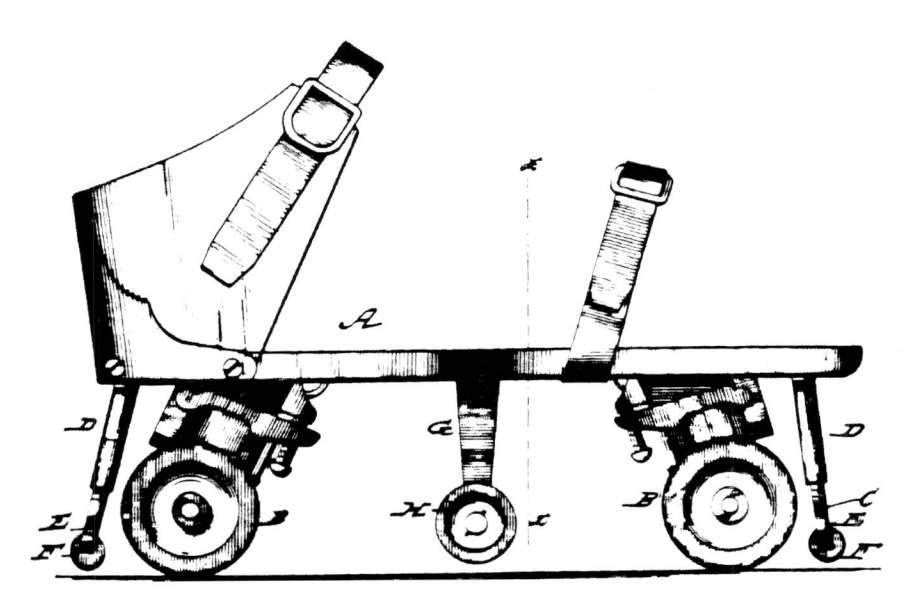

Brix Roller Skate, 1884

4 The Boom Period
1880-1910

At The Rink, 1885

Roller skating boomed during the 1880s. The American industrial machine, always ready to invest in a new fad, began producing roller skates by the thousands. Several brand name skates were on the market; usually each brand had several models to choose from. The skate companies also operated roller rinks to promote roller skating and sell their skates. Roller skating gained in popularity and rink operators advertised it as "a healthful sport and that a well ordered roller skating rink is a very commendable social experience for the youth."

The basic skate of the 1880s had the Plimpton type action and were strapped or clamped onto the shoe both front and back. The wheels were made of wood or metal and had a loose ball or pin type bearings to facilitate the roll. The plates were made of wood or metal. Skates designed for rink use were called "parlour" skates or "club" skates.

Let's take an excursion into the past and study an imaginary skater living in the 1880s in a large metropolitan city in the Eastern United States (this story taken from Alfred Smith, *Spalding's Manual of Roller Skating*, 1884). It is spring and this particular young man, named Robert, is looking for an amusement to take his girlfriend, Jane, to for the afternoon. In the newspaper there is an article advertising a new roller skating parlour, The Roller Palace, that just recently opened nearby. That's it! He decides to take his young lady out for an afternoon of fun on wheels.

It is Saturday afternoon when he picks her up in his horse drawn carriage. The skating session begins at two o'clock in the afternoon. The Roller Palace is not far from Jane's home. As he pulls into the entrance, an attendant takes the horse and leads it to a nearby area. He will watch the horse and carriage while they go inside the rink to skate. The lot is full and this is an indication that the session will, as usual, be crowded.

Robert walks around to assist Jane from the carriage and then escorts her to the entrance where he pays the admission: Adults 25 cents, children under twelve, 10 cents, this included skates.

After passing the admission teller they enter a large carpeted lobby. The decor is red and gold with white trims and curtains. There are seats all around the lobby to rest on. Straight ahead is the skating floor, a wooden surface 85' x 190', with a wooden fence all around it to assist beginners. An aisle goes down either side of the floor and there are seats there also. There is also a spectators balcony where the non-skaters can watch the action. There is a high vaulted ceiling with no support beams on the wooden skating surface. At the far end of the building is a stage. From this platform a thirty piece brass band performs. It is under the direction of Professor A. Austin, a cornetist of no "mean note," and the band plays for the entire two hour session. Popular music, polkas, marches, and waltzes are performed. The band plays well and adds a lot to the enjoyment of the skaters and the spectators. Waltz numbers remain popular and the good skaters imitate ballroom waltzing around the floor.

After listening to the band for a few minutes, they go to the skate room to obtain their skates. An attendant recommends solid shoes or boots and asks what size shoe they need and then finds the proper size skates. He gives the skates to another employee, the skate boy, who works for tips. After escorting them to a fitting area, the skate boy attaches the skates using straps, being careful not to cut off blood circulation to the feet. They skate for almost an hour before tiring to the point of exhaustion. Time for some refreshment at the soda fountain located in the lobby. Robert takes Jane for a cool drink. While sitting in the lobby on a red cushioned seat, they see a poster with the 1880's Rink Rules on display:

1. Skating begins at the sound of the gong and ceases at two strokes of the gong.
2. No smoking allowed, except in the smoking room in the lobby.
3. Gentlemen will not soil the floor with chewing tobacco.
4. Crowding, loud talking, or other rude or noisy demonstrations will not be permitted.
5. No one shall stand, not even for a moment, on the skating surface, or as to obstruct the view of spectators seated at the railing.
6. See that the skate strap buckles are on the outside of the shoe.
7. Never cut through the center of the skating floor; always follow the direction of the skaters.
8. Spitting or throwing of any substance on the surface is dangerous and will not be permitted.
9. Going up and down stairs on skates is strictly prohibited.
10. No stick, cane, string, or similar object should be carried onto the floor.
11. In skating around the circuit, all will observe a uniform speed and direction, taking great care not to interfere with others.
12. No skater should stop on the circuit, except to assist a lady.

It is little wonder roller skating became such a popular amusement for youths seeking wholesome activities!

The gong sounds two strokes and all the skaters clear the floor. The band plays a magnificent fanfare and it is announced that Professor Alfred Smith will present an exhibition of "fancy and scientific" skating. Mr. Smith, a professional skater, has toured the United States and Europe doing tricks on skates. He does a five minute demonstration to music of various dance steps, leaps into the air, performs figure skating, and fast skating both forward and backward.

After the exhibition, it is announced that Professor Smith will be residing there for a number of weeks throughout summer to give skating instructions to those interested in learning fancy and scientific skating and that a competition would be held at the Roller Palace before the end of his stay. Robert, most impressed with the athletic skill of Professor Smith, decides to come again to see him about lessons. Even if he did not win the competition in August, he would be a far superior skater to most, and make Jane very proud of him.

The next day, Robert goes back to the Roller Palace and finds Professor

Smith practicing figure skating in the center of the rink. He is amazed at the ease and grace that Smith has in doing such difficult moves. Robert remembers back to yesterday when he saw Smith's exhibition. Smith had done a heel split and leaned over so that his face nearly touched the floor and then maneuvered to pick up a handkerchief from the floor with only his teeth. He remembers the comedy imitation of a man learning how to skate and his very fast imitation of a locomotive.

"How wonderful it would be to execute these tricks," Robert says to himself. Then, looking up, he sees Alfred Smith skating toward him.

"Hello there young man. What can I do for you?" Mr. Smith asks in a friendly deep voice.

"I am interested in learning fancy and scientific skating such as I saw you do yesterday in the afternoon session," Robert replies.

"Do you have your own skates?" Smith asks.

"No, Sir."

Robert follows Mr. Smith to the lobby and into a side room marked "Skate Shoppe." In this room are new skates and all sorts of skating accessories for sale. Mr. Smith tells Robert that before he could learn the fancy skating tricks he must have good quality skates and equipment. He says the strap on skates were fine for session use but in fancy skating, skaters need special boots and skates since the straps break easily from the strain put on them. Smith hands Robert a price list of the skates that Roller Palace had in the "Skate Shoppe" (see to the right). Robert is amazed to see the variety of equipment available and the cost of good equipment. Fortunately, he is financially well off and the cost is not a problem. Certainly this was a rich man's sport. The poor can not afford to spend the twenty dollars for top equipment.

At Professor Smith's recommendation, Robert orders the Winslow Vineyard series, model H.C., and a pair of skating boots to match. He orders two pairs of good quality boxwood wheels with Richardson Ball Bearings, a pocket oiler, a skating cap, and a skate satchel for carrying his equipment. Professor Smith says that the skates would be ready in two days and that then he could begin lessons.

During the weeks that followed, Mr. Smith coached Robert in the art of fancy and scientific skating. Robert began with the easier movements, forward and backward edges, then learning two foot and one foot turns. Mr. Smith showed him the "Dutch Roll" step, named after the ice skaters in Holland who used it so frequently. Using the Dutch Roll step, Robert develops straight and fast progress around the floor. He learned the outside back edge with cross in back roll and the lap foot circle both to the right and the left.

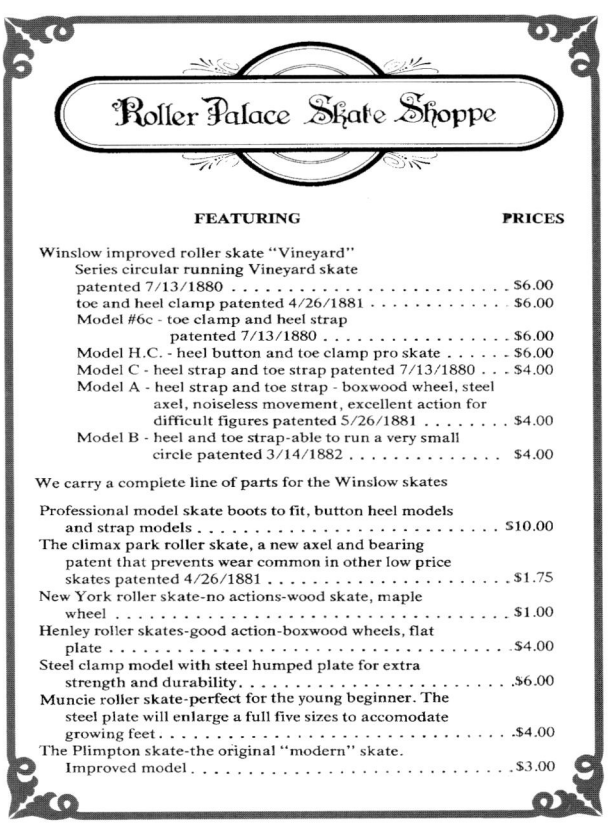

Roller Palace Skate Shoppe

FEATURING	PRICES
Winslow improved roller skate "Vineyard" Series circular running Vineyard skate patented 7/13/1880	$6.00
toe and heel clamp patented 4/26/1881	$6.00
Model #6c - toe clamp and heel strap patented 7/13/1880	$6.00
Model H.C. - heel button and toe clamp pro skate	$6.00
Model C - heel strap and toe strap patented 7/13/1880	$4.00
Model A - heel strap and toe strap - boxwood wheel, steel axel, noiseless movement, excellent action for difficult figures patented 5/26/1881	$4.00
Model B - heel and toe strap-able to run a very small circle patented 3/14/1882	$4.00
We carry a complete line of parts for the Winslow skates	
Professional model skate boots to fit, button heel models and strap models	$10.00
The climax park roller skate, a new axel and bearing patent that prevents wear common in other low price skates patented 4/26/1881	$1.75
New York roller skate-no actions-wood skate, maple wheel	$1.00
Henley roller skates-good action-boxwood wheels, flat plate	$4.00
Steel clamp model with steel humped plate for extra strength and durability	$6.00
Muncie roller skate-perfect for the young beginner. The steel plate will enlarge a full five sizes to accomodate growing feet	$4.00
The Plimpton skate-the original "modern" skate. Improved model	$3.00

These were all considered "plain" movements, "fancy" movements were combinations of plain movements and turns. The first of the "fancy" movements Robert learned was the serpentine, or changes of edge named for the snake like movement and tracing. Executed as one foot and two foot movements, forward and backward, the serpentine movement could also be done as a circle or a circle eight.

Left inside outside forwards
LIOF

ROIF

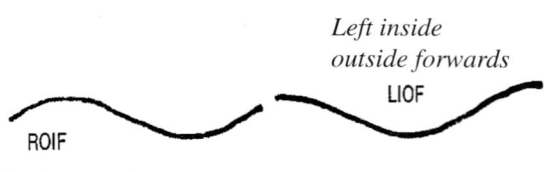

Right outside inside forwards

Robert learned the eight changes of edge and then double changes of edge sometimes with turns.

He executed figure eights on all four edges, and X-roll forward and backward, and also the "one foot" eight (paragraph eight), two circles with a single push.

Clover Figures

The "Three" or "Heart" figure and double threes or "clover" figures Robert executed on all edges. Variations of these were also possible.

Flying threes, the most athletic of the three turn movements as one must leap from one foot to the other, is considered quite "dashing" when done at high speed.

The graceful position of the "spread eagle" became one of Robert's favorite positions. These were done either upright or with forward and backward body leans.

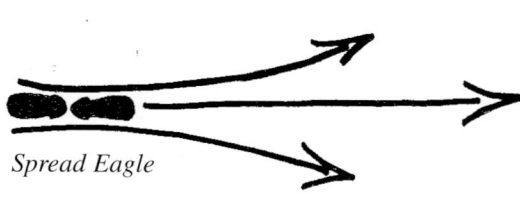

Spread Eagle

One of Smith's best moves was the "Locomotive." He began with a forward serpentine on the right, with the left foot assisting with side pushes from behind. First pushing from the right and then the left side of the skating foot. The effect is a perfect imitation of a steam locomotive building up speed. A "Double Locomotive" is possible by changing and making the right foot push and the left foot serpentine after each sequence. Single and double locomotives are also done in the same manner skating backward.

Robert also learned the "On to Richmond," a movement that Mr. Smith used frequently to add humor to a routine. While skating forward on the left foot, stretched the right foot out to its fullest extent in front, then crossed in front of the left, very wide and setting on an outside edge. This gave the humorous effect of skating one direction but actually traveling in the other direction. The "Reverse on to Richmond" consisted of the same principle except one skates backward and crosses in back with the free leg.

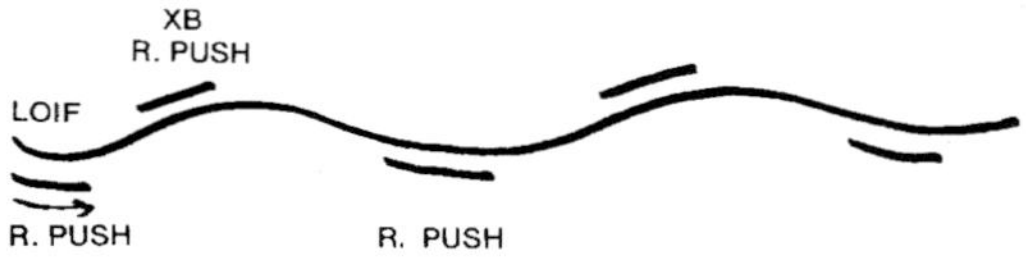

XB
R. PUSH
LOIF
R. PUSH   R. PUSH

Locomotive

Next, Robert learned more athletic roller skating feats. Smith showed him the "toe step" spins (toe pivots, placing the toe of one boot on the floor and pivoting around it), the two foot spins, and the one foot spins. There were twelve toe steps to learn, but these were not difficult since most of the weight was on the toe of the boot. Robert also learned combinations of toe steps and toe dancing (dance steps done on the toes alone). There are eight one foot spins, all of these are started on an edge, but Mr. Smith taught Robert that the proper exit was always to a flat (a straight line). On the LOF (left outside front) spin, Robert learned to "force" the spin by placing the right leg over the left knee and gradually close the feet together to create a fast rotation. On the RIF (right inside forward) spin Mr. Smith instructed him to rotate his head and shoulders to the left and stretch the free leg behind and across to assist the spin. These techniques were used to assist rotation due to the poor roll of the wheels. Skaters did not follow good modern upright form back then and they forced the edges to gain speed on spins. No skater executed sit or camel spins at this time.

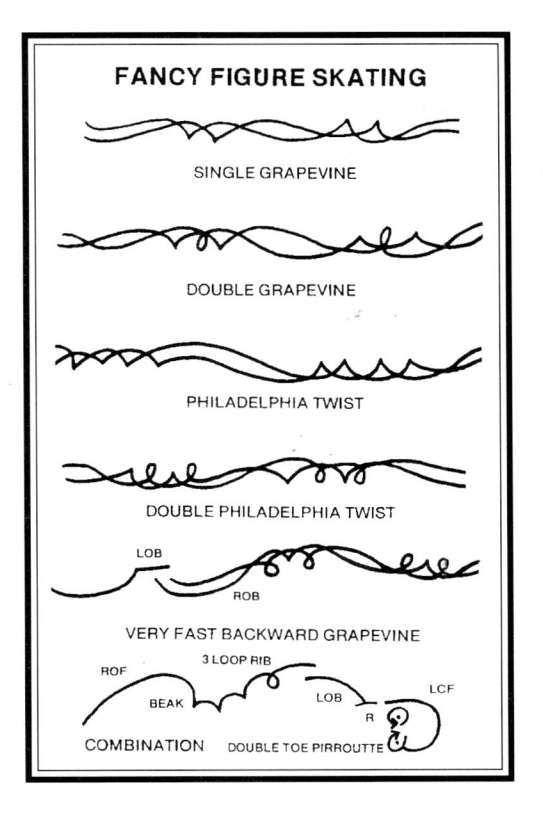

One foot loops were figures done either open or intertwined, practiced separately from the more circular "Ringlet" figures.

One of the hardest items in artistic skating consisted of the very difficult "grapevine" movement, adapted from ice skating. Accomplished on two feet, the diagram to the right traces the movements. Along the same lines was a move called the "Philadelphia Twist" and the "Double Philadelphia Twist," invented and made popular by ice skaters in that city. Starting forward, the feet crossed in a scissors movement, and while in the cross position the skater executed a two foot three turn. For the "double," the skater executed the same movement backwards, a cross-twist-turn to complete 360 degrees.

Professor Smith then instructed Robert to skate very fast and assume the famous pose of the "winged god Mercury." Skating on a forward edge, he raised his right foot and carried it behind him with toe pointed down, the right arm extended in front and the left arm to the side. Called the "Double Mercury," the move became very popular among partners. Each partner executes "The Mercury" side by side in perfect matching and unison.

Partner skating was also called "combination skating." Usually two men participated, since, as Mr. Smith pointed out, the more athletic moves proved too strenuous for a lady with the long cumbersome and restrictive dresses that women wore in the 1880s. Combination skating included "toe steps" holding one hand with your partner, and "The Flying Scud," where both partners faced each other and joined hands. Each alternately executed a three and a mohawk and the team "flies" down the rink building up momentum. These movements, called "field movements," since there is no prescribed pattern and the team will travel in which ever direction chance dictates.

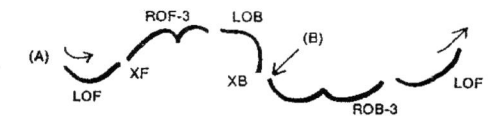

Flying Scud

Four well advanced skaters could execute very intricate figures in perfect unison. These very fancy Fours combinations reminded one of a square dance on skates.

Professor Smith introduced Robert to leaping into the air and turning a half rotation. The complete full turn jump was considered most difficult and the one and one-half turn jumps were not done at this time. Skaters take off and land on either one foot or two feet. Mr. Smith encouraged Robert to leap to the fullest height possible to achieve his rotation.

Mr. Smith completed this course with the mastery on the "Bishop's Eight," a difficult fancy figure popular in competition at the time.

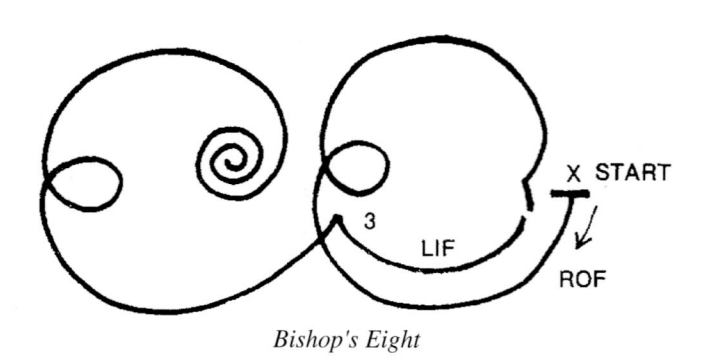

Bishop's Eight

Robert practiced every day for the entire summer to learn all of these moves. He practiced diligently and accomplished much. In August, the Roller Palace published and passed out the requirements for the competition to all entrants. Though free to enter, you had to be recommended by Professor Smith as qualified to compete. The winner received a solid gold medal as the prize.

The program was taken from that recommended by the Spalding Company in their official *Roller Polo and Fancy Skating Guide*, 1896:

1. Plain skating forward and backward.
2. Lap foot - as a field movement and a circle movement.
3. Outside Forward (OF) edges.
4. Outside Back (OB) edges.
5. Inside Forward (IF) edges.
6. Inside Back (IB) edges.
7. Cross roll forward.
8. Cross roll backward.
9. Change of edge forward.
10. Change of edge backward.
11. a. "On to Richmond" - cross forward while skating forward.
    b. "Reverse on to Richmond" - cross back while skating backward.
12. Locomotive - forward, backward, single or double.
13. A waltz step - done to music.
14. Spread eagle - inside and outside edges.
15. Figure threes:
    a. Inside and outside on the field and on the eight, including "flying threes."
    b. Double three - on the eight - inside and outside edges.
16. Grapevines and the Philadelphia Twist.
17. Toe and heel movements - embracing toe steps, heel steps, toe spins (pirouettes), movements on both toes.
18. Single flat foot spins, and double whirls (two foot spins).
19. Serpentines - forward and backward - with foot in front and in back.
20. Figure eight on one foot forward (modern #24).
21. Figure eight on one foot backward (modern #25).
22. Change of edge, single and double.
23. Loops - inside and outside edges, simple eight and combinations of loops.
24. Ringlets - inside and outside edges, simple eight and combinations

of ringlets.
25. Specialities, embracing original and peculiar movements.
26. General display of combined movements at the option of the contestant (Freestyle).

On the day of the competition, the Roller Palace filled to capacity. The publicity of the event was well done and each entrant had his own personal cheering section. Professor Smith and people knowledgeable in dancing, theater, and ice skating judged the competition. The competition required each contestant to execute every movement, each movement done by a contestant before moving to the next items to give the judges a chance to compare the performances. If a contestant could not attempt a particular movement he was disqualified. Thus, by the last ten movements only the best remained. Robert was one of the last. Items twenty-five and twenty-six, original movements and exhibitions would finally decide the champion. This competition began the freestyle skating.

Robert's free exhibition consisted a field exercise with a variety of good movements. However, the first prize went to another, the experienced champion, winner of several previous competitions. Robert realized, though not up to the caliber of this fine skater and gentleman, he made a good showing for his first time in competition. Rink managers held fancy skating competitions of this type during the 1880-1910 period, as well as speed skating races and roller polo matches to promote skating at various rinks. The specialties and peculiar movements became part of the repertoire of the skaters and this is how content was developed for freestyle.

These contests were not always sanctioned by any national body and thus many claimed to National and World Champion titles. The movements were not standardized and there were few trained judges to officiate. The United States Figure Skating Association was not established until 1921, and even ice competition was spotty and disorganized.

Jesse Darling

5 SKATING ASSOCIATIONS

James L. Plimpton started the New York Roller Skating Association which was affiliated with his rinks and skate company. The NYRSA that opened up the Atlantic House skating rink in 1866 and international ties were made with the British and other European countries.

In 1886 F.P. Goode, J.B. Story, and other ice skaters formed the U.S. National Amateur Skating Association. The National Skating Association (NSA) of Great Britain was formed in 1879, sponsoring competitions and tests on ice and later on roller skates. American skaters followed the NSA lead for many years.

Allen T. Blanchard of Chicago, Illinois, first officially organized roller and ice skating nationally in America. Blanchard, an ice speed and figure champion, a referee, and a judge, was referred to as "Pop" and recognized as the father of organized skating in America. He helped found the International Skating Union of America (ISU) in 1891, and he represented the Western Skating Association. The ISU divided the United States into three sections: Eastern Association, New England Association, and Western Association. Two additional Canadian sections were also included. This association wrote rules of entry, rules of amateur status, annual dues, registered rinks, and championship rules for speed and artistic skating on both ice and rollers in America and Canada. Figure and speed skating championships were held annually but popular interest lay in speed until 1914.

Julian T. Fitzgerald

The Western Skating Association became organized under the leadership of Julian T. Fitzgerald of Chicago in the early 1900's. Actually mid-western group members lived west of the Allegheny Mountains, including skaters from Ohio, Indiana, West Virginia, Indiana, Illinois, Wisconsin, Minnesota, Iowa, and western Pennsylvania. Little organized skating occurred west of the Mississippi River. There was a comprehensive program of competitive rules and regulations (1906-1920). The roller speed championships had races for 1/2 mile, 3/4 mile, 1 mile, 2 mile, 3 mile, 5 mile, and 10 mile. Figure skating was based on plain skating and fancy skating movements outlined by Allen T. Blanchard of the ISU.

By 1921, there was enough interest in figure skating on ice for the formation of the United States Figure Skating Association (USFSA). The ISU allowed USFSA to control figure skating. Roller skating, however, was not sufficiently organized at this time to be included, only seven ice clubs made up the original USFSA roster.

In 1907 an American roller skater, Chester Park, went to Liverpool, England, and built an American style roller skating rink. The skating boom of the 1880s had died in America and

Construction of Skating Floor, 1925

American roller skate companies were looking for markets. Park represented the Samual Winslow Roller Skate Company. He installed a maple parquet floor in an old building using good rink management techniques to operate the business. Park became very successful, and started a roller skating boom in England.

Roller skating clubs began forming all over Europe. The British started an Amateur Hockey Association in 1905. Speed and hockey meets were held in Europe from 1906 to 1914. Before World War I, a movement started to organize on an international level, but with the war most rinks closed. After the war ended, the Jazz Era caused many former rinks to re-open as dance halls and jazz clubs. The NSA was still active in England though the roller skating craze died down on the continent.

Victor J. Brown & Fred A. Martin

The Federation International de Patinage a Roulette (FIPR) formed in 1924 in Montreux, Switzerland to promote hockey, speed, and figure skating. Fred Renkewitz and Otto Mayer founded the FIPR, with Mayer serving as its first Secretary. Mayer also served as Chancellor of the International Olympic Committee at that time. In Belgium in 1941, the first National Roller Skating Championship in a European country was organized. After World War II, Italy, Germany, and Belgium held a European Roller Skating Championships in 1946.

The Arena Gardens Roller Skating Rink in Detroit, Michigan, held in 1937 the first National Roller Speed Skating Championship where seventeen rink owners formed the RSROA (Roller Skating Rink Operators Association) to promote the roller skating business and sport in America. After the final events of the competition, operators and managers walked down Woodward Avenue to the Casa Loma Restaurant as guests of Fred Martin, the meet host. Martin, a World Professional Speed skater during his youth, wanted to discuss their common problems in promoting the roller skating business in America, regulation and protection of roller skating contests for amateurs, and to act as a governing body for the sport. These men believed that if skating was to be a successful sport, it must also be a successful business. A competitive skater must have the best rink facilities, ample practice time, quality skates, and good instructors and coaches all in addition to physical talent, to become a champion. During the meeting, Victor J. Brown, a rink owner and sports promoter from Newark, New Jersey, was elected the President and Fred Martin the Secretary-Treasurer. The group each donated one dollar and Fred Martin took the meager funds back to his office to begin the work. A single drawer in Martin's desk became the first RSROA National Office, a group which grew throughout the following years into a world reknown skating association.

RSROA - THE INTRODUCTION OF INTERNATIONAL STYLE ON ROLLER SKATES IN AMERICA

Although rinks held local and regional competitions throughout the 1920s and 1930s, no national organization existed to assist the sport of roller skating until 1937. Fancy skating was done on vaudeville stages and on table platforms in circus acts, competitive skating generally restricted to speed or marathon endurance races.

Fred Martin, Vic Brown, and Perry Rawson proved instrumental in introducing roller dance and figure skating to the United States. Martin was then the Manager of the Arena Gardens Roller Rink in Detroit, Michigan, and Vic Brown, owned the New Dreamland Rink in Newark, NJ.

Perry Rawson

Rawson, a skater from the New York area and a retired stock broker, had the time and money to devote to his hobby. While traveling across England in 1937, Rawson saw European roller skaters doing the same movements as ice skaters. Many of these skaters did ice skating in the winter and roller skating in the summer.

Perry Rawson sent a letter to Fred Martin of the new RSROA and told him about the wonderful dancing on roller skates that he saw. Perry felt this "artistic" skating would go over well in America. He offered to take movies to show the RSROA the possibilities of dance and figure skating. Rawson persuaded Martin so he made him chairman of the RSROA Dance Committee. Rawson introduced and promoted this international style dance and figure skating in RSROA member rinks.

Rawson arranged a tour for some of the finest skaters of the time to come to America and give live demonstrations at RSROA rinks. Jimmy and Joan Lidstone, the British and European dance champions, and Billy Watson, an English figure skater, were invited as Rawson's guests to the United States in 1938 to give exhibitions. The Lidstones were the foremost roller dance team in the world at that time. Mr. Rawson continued his personal interest in the sport and traveled extensively, learning dances and techniques of international skating in North America and Europe. He wrote numerous articles, judges notes on dances, and skating manuals to assist the American skaters in the new type of roller skating. Some dancing on skates had been done in America, but of the "jitterbug" type, not nationally known dances but local "jive steps" done to fast tempo music.

Jimmy & Joan Lidstone, Billy Watson

Ralph "Duke" Hudson of Skateland Rink in Denver, Colo., July 1942.

Earl & Inez Van Horn, 1933

Throughout the 1940s, Perry Rawson's guidance helped introduce and develop the "American" style of dance skating. Rawson built a small roller rink on his estate in Asbury Park, NJ, which he called his skating laboratory. Rawson invited pros and amateurs to visit his estate and discuss topics on skating. He also wrote the first instruction books on basic skating, dance skating, and dance diagrams for roller skaters.

Several other leaders emerged in these formative years of artistic skating. R. H. "Duke" Hudson, a professional skater of note on rollers in Chicago and later in Memphis, Tennessee, could execute the most advanced school figures equally well on rollers as those executed on ice. He encouraged many skaters to convert from ice to rollers. Earl and Inez Van Horn, well known acrobatic skaters on stage in the 1930s, became excellent teachers in both associations in New York in the 1940s. Louis Bargmann, an amateur from Chicago, turned professional in Washington, D.C. in 1940. He wrote articles, judged, and taught the International Style in that area. Fred Freeman from Massachusetts promoted the large class method of teaching dance and figures. Large numbers of skaters took lessons to learn the basics of the International Style all over the country. There were also professional and judges seminars introducing the Gold Medal Dances and Figures to amateurs and pros. Victor Brown, Fred Martin, and the original founders of the RSROA were responsible for the financial assistance, encouragement, and improving the standards of rinks, teachers, judges, and skaters.

The year 1942 was a bleak one for the American skater, as the United States entered World War II and dedicated their young men and total economy to a war time effort. During the war, roller skaters became involved in a dispute with the Amateur Athletic Union (AAU) and the resulting in a split into two major national skating organizations, the RSROA and the United States Amateur Roller Skating Association (USARSA).

The dispute was actually between the RSROA, the controlling body of competitive roller skating since its formation in 1937, and the AAU, the national group which controlled all amateur sports in conjunction with the Olympic Committee. The actual decision makers of roller skating were professionals and rink owners, not the amateur skater, although the RSROA felt they acted in the best interest of the sport. This was intolerable at this time due to the amateur purist attitudes of amateurism during the Avery Brundage era, who was President of the United States and International Olympic Committee.

In 1941, several non-member rinks filed complaints against the RSROA as did a journalist with a New York newspaper interested in sponsoring skating events. These complaints were sent to the American Skating Union (ASU), a national organizational that administered all forms of amateur skating in America. The ASU was closely aligned with the AAU.

The RSROA resigned from the ASU, and continued to conduct its amateur competitive events, holding a National Championship in 1942. Another group of skaters, believing that amateur skaters should administer the sport, formed a second roller skating association, the United States Amateur Roller Skating Association (USARSA). For the next thirty years, these two organizations administered two National Championships. Two styles of skating developed in America as the groups did not closely communicate in the development of the sport.

Finally in 1971-72, after all the initial disputants were dead, the United States Federation of Amateur Roller Skaters (USFARS), the RSROA amateurs, and the USARSA negotiated a merger and American skaters once again came under one National organization called the United States Confederation of Roller Skating (USAC/RS). USAC/RS (now USA Roller Skating) governs all aspects of the competitive amateur sport and works with the United States Olympic Committee (USOC) to develop roller skating to new levels of excellence as a sport. USA Roller Skating holds competitive skating competition in both American and International Style artistic events, speed skating on quads and in-line skates, and hard ball, puck, and North American style hockey. Roller skaters were also included in the 1978 Sports Act and they participated in the Pan Am Games since 1979.

The 1970's were a decade of experimentation, numerous rule revisions, and stylistic changes. In the 1980's American skaters began to dominate International competition in speed and artistic events. USOC training has been made available to roller skaters at the training center in Colorado Springs, Colorado. Roller skaters have been participants in the U.S. Olympic Festival, the World Games, and the Pan American Games. In 1992, roller hockey (hardball) was an exhibition sport in the Summer Olympic Games in Barcelona, Spain.

Society of Roller Skating Teachers of America

6 ORIGINS OF SKATE DANCES

Elsbeth Muller, 1941

Dancing to music on skates can be traced back with certainty to the American ballet teacher, figure skater, and inventor of freestyle, Jackson Haines. While visiting in Vienna, Austria, in 1865, Haines taught the city's population the joy of dancing the waltz on skates. A band assembled and skaters waltzed for hours. If Haines did not invent the waltz on skates, he certainly made it the popular thing to do in Europe in the late 1860s.

The first waltz steps merely mimic the actual ballroom technique. This was a very awkward movement to do on skates, more like walking than gliding. Some members of the British nobility, who skated in the Swiss resorts in the winter, were among the first to develop the three turn type waltz step in the 1880s. The three turn waltz was also done in Nova Scotia, Canada, as early as 1885. The first official public performance of the three turn waltz step was in Paris, in 1894. A French professional skater, Monsieur Richard, did a skate dance exhibition at the "Palais de Glace." Several English skaters in attendance saw his step and took it back to England.

The British skaters were very stiff and technical as opposed to the free flowing Viennese style of Jackson Haines. Members of the National Skating Association of Great Britain (ice and roller), the British skating establishment, felt that this European dancing craze (1870-1890), was not good for serious figure skaters. It was too social and not a serious sport. If a team danced nearby, often a figure skater purposely got in the way to show his disdain for this "Continental" waltzing. The name remains Continental Waltz to this day.

The march dances originated on skates, not in the ballroom. Franz Scholler in Austria invented the 10 Step (that is the corner steps of the modern 14 Step) in 1887. Called the "Scholler Marsch" (march), couples skated as either a 2/4 march or a 3/4 fast waltz.

In 1907, George and Elsbeth Muller, brother and sister waltz champions from Germany, learned the Scholler 10 Step from a visiting Austrian skater in Berlin. Near that same time, they also learned the "14 Step" version of the dance. The Mullers, excellent waltzers, learned the new dances very quickly. From Berlin, the Scholler March spread all over Europe to England and America. The Mullers later moved to the United States and turned professional, teaching and inventing ice and roller dances in Boston and St. Louis. Later, Elsbeth Muller taught roller and ice skating in Detroit, Michigan.

After the world wide success of the 10 Step, the Viennese skater, Karl Schreiter, introduced another Austrian dance in 1909. Inspired by an Austrian folk dance, it proved a very difficult step to master and became popular among the advanced dancers. Originally called the "Side by Side 14 Step," many confused it with the "Scholler 14 Step," so another name was used--The Kilian. The Kilian steps were the same as the modern dance except that sometimes a couple skated a once around pattern, creating deep edges and difficult rotation problems. At first skaters performed the Kilian with a mohawk turn rather than the cross in back choctaw (cross toe

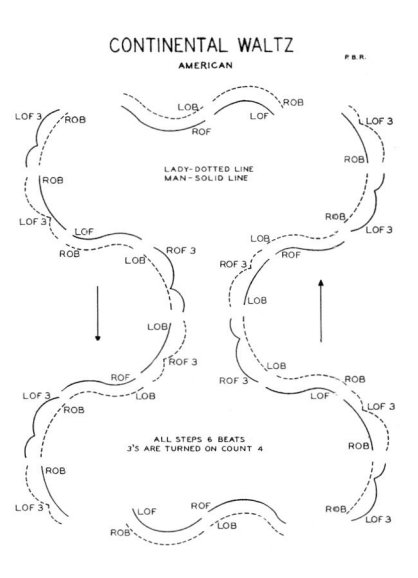

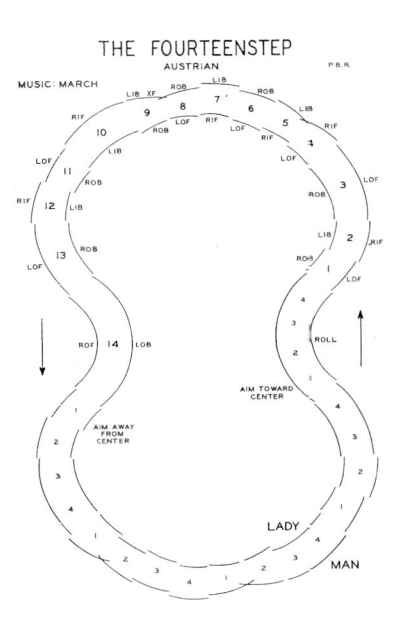

THE KILIAN
AUSTRIAN
MUSIC: MARCH

cut-off) step used today.

By 1930, the only dances known in America were the waltz and the Scholler Marches, dances done on rollers and ice. In 1932, an American, G. E. B. Hill, went to England on a visit. A skater himself, Hill noticed a high proficiency of skating the waltz, 14 Step, and figures. He also saw a new dance unknown in America--The Tango. Hill returned to the United Stated after learning the dance and wrote an article on it in *Skating*, the USFSA magazine (1932). American roller and ice skaters quickly learned this dance created by Trudy Harris and Paul Krechow. The dance was diagrammed as a boarder dance and the timing was similar to the modern international style dance version.

After 1932, the British dance trend was set for the next decade. The German skaters were more interested in figure and pairs skating. The Americans tended to follow the British trends pretty closely. The ice and roller dance teams in England demanded more and better quality dances. Dance specials were included in every club skate, but there were only three standard dances to do: Waltz, 14 Step, and Tango.

Robert Dench and Lesley Turner, his partner, invented The Blues in 1934. Dench wrote a book on dance and pairs skating with his wife Rosemarie Stewart. Both were stars in the original Ice Capades show in the 1940s, and they remained with the show as choreographers and production coordinators. Many of the Gold Dances we do today were invented in England in the 1930s.

Joseph Carroll, an outstanding teacher in New York in the 1930s, wrote the Carroll Swing Fox Trot and the Carroll Tango dances for the American skaters. Another pro from New York, Katie Schmidt, taught at the same rink as World Champion figure skater Willie Boeckl. She wrote the Iceland Tango and they collaborated on the Schmidt-Boeckl dance which was popular in the 1940s. Kenneth Chase did not write the Chase Waltz. He was the 1942 RSROA Figure champion killed in action during WW II. Fred Bergin, Connie Umbach, and Betty Jane Yarrington wrote the dance following Chase's death as a dedication to him. Inez Van Horn of the Mineola Rink, N.Y. wrote the Collegiate, a skating version of the popular dance of the same name. The corner had only four steps, but Perry Rawson added two more corner steps to make the dance we know today. Van Horn wrote the Collegiate for session skaters to help them learn correct mohawk turns.

The Evolution of American Style Dance

Since all that was known of dance skating in America in 1938 came from the Lidstone exhibitions or from Perry Rawson's interpretations of ice skaters, how did the American style of dance evolve? The evolution involved several factors, not the least of which was Hitler, who through starting World

Kenny Chase & Partner

War II, isolated the U.S. from other skating countries.

The Lidstones came to the U.S. in 1938, the same year that hostilities first began on the continent, eventually involving the principal skating countries of the 1930s: England, Germany, and Italy. The German skaters were basically figure and pairs, the British dance and figures, and the Italians speed. Many ice skated in the winter and roller skated in the summers. The British had indoor roller rinks and were more dedicated roller skaters, although some did switch skates like the Germans. The Lidstones, though the European dance champions, their style of skating was less like ice dance, skating with an upright posture and a smoother flow to their strokes than an ice - roller combination team. Jimmy Lidstone attributed this to the fact that he and his sister were not figure skaters, as the Germans were, and that they concentrated on dance with some figure skating.

Using the Lidstones as a guide, but also adding his own techniques to roller skating, Perry Rawson became very influential in developing the American style. His idea was that a dance team should have power, but not let it show by violent pushing. He developed the American style of parallel progressive stroking, where a team could move around the floor in a smooth, almost effortless style. He convinced some of the leading RSROA pros that this method better suited roller skates. Further, he persuaded many against copying ice skating techniques as such techniques rarely suited roller skaters. Techniques of American style roller skating consisted of an upright posture, smooth stroking, very little bouncing, heel to heel aim in mohawks, and the border dance baseline concept. Earlier dance teams skated slowly, but many, such as the team of Clifford Schattenkirk and Bettie Jennings from Seattle, Washington, began to skate with good speed and flow. By 1947, skaters accepted their faster style of dance as they won the American Senior title.

The war itself isolated Americans from Europeans and the independent development of American style dance occurred without outside influence. Also, due to the RSROA - AAU dispute, very little communication with United States ice skaters took place. By 1948, the die was cast and the American dance style, introduced in 1938 and developed by RSROA pros and champions, was quite different than dancing on either ice or European-International Style roller skaters.

After World War II ended and European skaters began competing again, dance events were included in the World competitions on ice in 1952. The dance events were judged in three parts; (1) compulsory dance, (2) original set pattern (OSP), (3) free dance, at the World Meet. Barbara Gallagher and Fred Ludwig from the Mineola Club in New York became the first post-WW II World Dance Champions in 1947. The Olympics did not include dance events until 1972.

Some of the top dance skaters of the 1950s became the leaders of the

Betty Jennings & Cliff Schattenkirk

modern roller skating movement: Bob and Joan LaBriola, Senior Dance champions 1950-1953; Gary Castro and Marilyn Roberts champions in 1955-1956; and Charles Wahlig with Miriam Centaro and Claire Farrell into late 1950s. LaBriola, Castro, and Wahlig have all been instrumental in the development of roller skating into the 1990's.

Linda Mottice Clemens and Adolf Wacker were the American dance champions seven consecutive times in the 1960s. Curt Craton later broke this string of victories skating with different partners in the 1980s.

The RSROA introduced Free Dance in the 1964 championships in order to prepare the skaters entering the World Championships. Though set up as a separate event, the same top Senior Dance teams usually won the placements. David Tassinari and Pat Fogerty Graney from Norwood, Massachusetts, won the first three years of the Free Dance event and generally set the style of the event since then. Linda Gyenese and Mike Crickmore, the 1969 and 1970 Free Dance champions, introduced the novelty style routine infusing humorous and serious moves. Many times an innovative or creative move is invented by accident. When Angie Famiano and David Golub practiced preparing their championship Free Dance routine, they slipped and caught each other in a special tango pose that became their signature move. Their coach, Jack Burton, realized what a great move this was and had them duplicate it and add it to their World Class routine. They went on to win the World title in 1983 and 1984. They are noted for their creative Free Dance and original set pattern routines that were well choreographed and well skated.

Even though excellent dancers, the RSROA teams, did not do well in World competition. In the 1960s the "American Style" of dance was not acceptable to the European dominated judges panel at the World meet. Therefore, in 1970, the United States International Competition (USIC) event was held at the American Championships. This new event, open to the Senior skaters and gold medalists in proficiency tests, was a competition based on European and World Meet rules designed to pick the best candidates for World competition, not necessarily the American Style National Champions. For example, the dance team of Baba Brooks and Bill Graf, winners of the USIC dance in 1970, never placed in Senior American Dance. They got fifth place at the World Meet in 1970, very good for a first time team at Worlds. Richard Horne and Jane Pankey became the USARSA Dance Champions and World Champions the same year. The World Team from the United States was made up of skaters from both the RSROA and USARSA until 1972. For the most part, because they were trained in the European International style, the USARSA

Adolph Wacker & Linda Mottice Clemens

Angie Famiano & David Golub

skaters placed higher, especially in dance. Since the merger of USFARS and USARSA in 1972, the United States has produced many World Champions and placements in World Dance competitions.

Richard Horne & Jane Pankey (1st Place) at the 1970 World Championships in Lincoln, Nebraska

7 THE ORIGINS OF FIGURE & FREE SKATING

Betty Lytle

As one observes a modern competition, with hundreds of anxious figure skaters preparing to test their skill against one another, the thought occurs: where did this figure skating sport come from? Since the first practical roller skate capable of executing curves and figures was not invented until the 1860's, the basic developments originated from ice skaters.

Early Figures (1840's)

In 1772, Lt. Robert Jones, a British Army Officer, wrote the first figure instruction book in English. He described the outside edge as a more artistic movement and the inner forward edge as more functional, used mostly for distance skating. Few considered backward skating as practical since many considered it a novelty movement. One of Jones' most interesting descriptions was the Heart (see above), called the "three turn" by 1795.

By the time of Louis XVI, figure skating was highly developed in France. Jean Garcin, skater and author, wrote a skating book entitled *Le Vrai Patineur* (The Real Skater) or "How To Skate With Grace," because of his concern with correct style and posture as well as the image produced on the ice. Garcin described 31 figures and gave them colorful names like Pas de Huit (ROF - right outside forward - figure eight), the Reverence (spread eagle), the Courtisane (OF - outside forward - three), the Nymphe (OB -outside back -eight), and the Jump of Zypher (a jump three).

Fancy Figures (1890)

During the 1840s, two Englishmen, H. E. Vandervell and Maxwell Witham, began a project to document all possible figures using the basic movements of that time, the edge, three, que, and loop, in various combinations. During the winter of 1860-61, Vandervell experimented with a one foot turn from inside forward to inside back. He named it the "rocking turn" because of the rocking motion created during its execution. This became the modern counter turn.

In 1878-81 two students from Oxford, Monier-Williams and Pidgeon, experimented with Vandervell's rocking turn in the reverse rotation. Pidgeon called it the "three quarter turn." Later the name changed to "reverse rocking turn," Vandervell's turn became called "counter rocking turn." Thus, in time these names shortened to the modern rocker and counter terminology.

The bracket (a one foot turn) was named for the shape of the figure that is traced. It was actually invented on roller skates by Max Witham in the late 1850s. There is evidence that the bracket was not popular on ice until 20 years later, when Witham published a diagram of the turn in 1880.

During the 1880s, skaters conducted figure competitions with school figures for eliminations and special figures for finals.

Austrian Advanced Figures (1897)

Many old ice skating books diagrammed some of these special figures of the 1880-1910 period.

Fancy figures never became popular to do on roller skates, as the whole intent is the picture left on the ice rather than the execution of the move. The importance of special figures is that these events were often used for inventing new turns, jumps, and spins. Often the skater was given a choice of doing either a special figure or a free skating exhibition in the finals.

Besides the 41 basic international figures, the RSROA added several new figures to the achievement test program. These were not the only additions to the figure schedule. At the Austrian Nationals in 1897, the figure skaters had to execute the basic 41 figures, and the "advanced" figures, and free style to qualify for World competition.

The American figure skaters on rollers followed the development of the ice sport and attempted to duplicate figures and free skating on wheels. During the 1930s, skaters used two types of skate adjustments, tight action and flexible action. By the early 1940s, the flexible action skater won the argument, since the more difficult figures, especially the loops, became much easier to do with a flexible action adjustment.

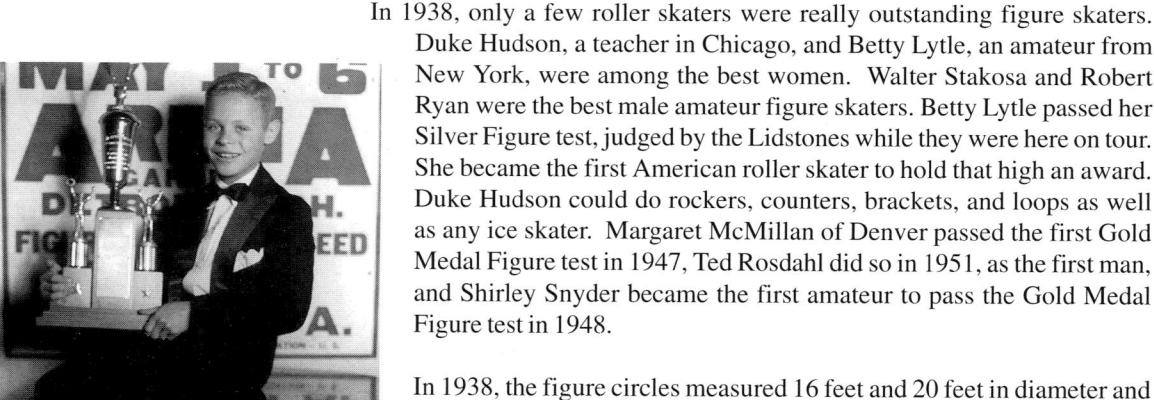

Walter Stakosa

In 1938, only a few roller skaters were really outstanding figure skaters. Duke Hudson, a teacher in Chicago, and Betty Lytle, an amateur from New York, were among the best women. Walter Stakosa and Robert Ryan were the best male amateur figure skaters. Betty Lytle passed her Silver Figure test, judged by the Lidstones while they were here on tour. She became the first American roller skater to hold that high an award. Duke Hudson could do rockers, counters, brackets, and loops as well as any ice skater. Margaret McMillan of Denver passed the first Gold Medal Figure test in 1947, Ted Rosdahl did so in 1951, as the first man, and Shirley Snyder became the first amateur to pass the Gold Medal Figure test in 1948.

In 1938, the figure circles measured 16 feet and 20 feet in diameter and were painted on the floor. Loops were done in rosin powder, until the 1950s, with no loop circles to follow. In 1970, the RSROA adopted the use of metric circles (5m and 6m) to conform to the World standards. During the 1940s, roller skating figure contests became all-around competitions. Each skater did figures for elimination and freestyle for finals, and judges named an all-around winner. In 1950, the RSROA split the competition into two different events and two champions were named, one for figures and one for freestyle.

Ted Rosdahl, 1944, Junior Boys Figure Champion

In 1980, the World Roller Skating meet split into two competitions, allowing each country to send figure and freestyle specialists, rather than an all-around skater to Worlds. This enabled a skater unable to do both events to compete at Worlds. Presently a figure, a freestyle, and an all-around (figure and freestyle combined) winner are named at the World Roller Skating Championships.

Tony St. Jacques reigned as a National Champion in Figures from 1977-1984. He won the senior event five times. The West German skaters dominated the men's figure event at the World level since 1937, but in 1983 Tony became the first American to win the FIRS (Federational Internationale de Roller Skating) World Figure event. He then won the National and World Figure title again in 1984. Since then the Americans have dominated the World Meet in figures including World Champions Kevin Carroll, Skip Clinton, Justin Bates, Steven Findley, Lynn Suwinski, and April Dayney.

Most freestyle content came from the fancy figure skating contests. After skating the basic school figures, each contestant could do their own fancy figure or some other trick to show their skill. A new movement was often named for the first skater to present an item at a major competition.

Tony St. Jacques

The sit spin, as mentioned earlier, was invented by Jackson Haines in the 1860s. The camel spin came much later, in the 1930s. It was called by some the arabesque spin, the airplane spin, and the parallel spin. The term "camel" meant a spin with poor posture (the ever present hump) but the nickname stuck and now all arabesque spins are called camels. Dick Button introduced the jump camel on ice in the 1940s and shortly thereafter roller skaters adopted it.

The axel jump was named for a Norwegian champion from the 1880s, Axel Paulsen. The story goes that he developed it while barrel jumping, and later presented it at the International Figure Skating Championship in 1882. Though another story tells that he jumped it over the backs of donkeys in exhibition. Paulsen later moved to the U.S. and skated in Minnesota. He owned a cigar store there and inspired the skaters in the area with his jumping.

The Salchow Jump is named for Ulrich Salchow, the Sweden, European, and World Champion, from 1900 to 1910. He always presented his jump after a three turn, still a popular technique today for roller skaters. The Wally (and later Toe Wally) jump was invented by Nathanial Wally, World Professional Champion of the 1930s. Willie Boeckl, World Champion from Austria in the 1920s, created the Boeckl jump.

Freestyle content on roller skates was not well done in the early years. By the 1930s fancy figures developed into modern free style routines. Roller skaters learned figures and freestyle in the 1940s from great champion skaters like Salchow, Wally, and Boeckl. The popular wooden wheels were a drawback for skaters, for they frequently broke or slipped in jumping. Lack of quality toe stops to assist in jumping further hampered skaters.

In the 1939 championships at the first RSROA Nationals, the senior

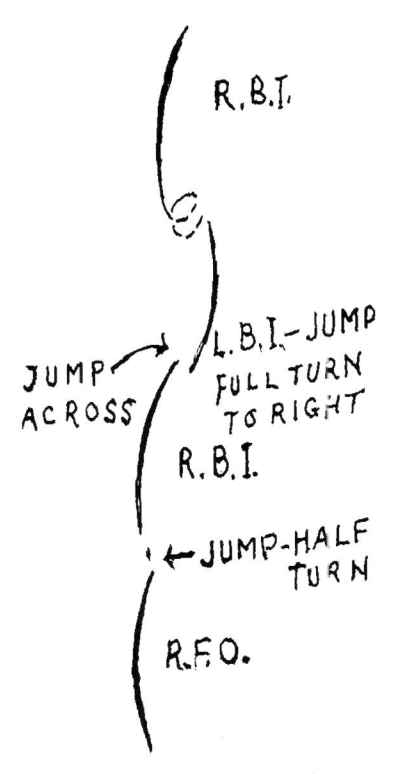

A footwork sequence drawn by Nathanial Wally, 1943

47

competitors could only perform the single revolution jumps. Outer back loop, salchow, and flip constituted the hardest jumps attempted. The men could only spin upright if at all. Bobby Ryan, the champion in 1941, accomplished a poor sit spin in 1940. In the Chicago area, two skaters introduced the most difficult content done on roller skates up to that time. Heddy Stenuf, a champion in Europe and a World and Olympic ice skater, lived in the Chicago area training under American coaches. Her pair's partner, Skippy Baxter, an American ice skater, was an excellent singles skater. Both were World Champion material on ice and could do excellent free style, even double jumps! They transferred their skating skill to roller skates with very little problem.

Heddy Stenuf, 1934

In 1939, Bobby Ryan was in the Chicago area judging the Illinois Championships. During the public session, he discussed the development of hard content and he mentioned that he was perfecting the Axel Paulsen jump for next year. Louis Bargmann, a novice skater at that time, told Ryan about a skater that could already do the axel and even a double salchow. Ryan, of course, refused to believe this, so Louis called out onto the floor to Skippy Baxter standing on the traffic line, "Hey, Skippy, do an axel!" Baxter did not have a good pair of freestyle skates, in fact he was wearing clamp on skates with street shoes, but pushed off forward from a stand still and did three axels in a series around the corner of the rink! Baxter, needless to say, was impressed by Ryan.

Jimmy Lidstone served as a naval officer during the war. His ship was torpedoed in the Atlantic and he spent five days adrift on a life raft before his rescue. He then spent several weeks in the New York area on leave. While in the New York area, he visited Perry Rawson's estate, Vic Brown's New Dreamland Rink, and gave exhibitions with Bobby Ryan, Melva Block, and Ann Manion at many New York rinks. In New York, he met the star of an ice show at the Roxy Theatre, Skippy Baxter. Lidstone became awed by Baxter's axel. To quote, "I was amazed at the perfection to which this young performer had brought the art of jumping on skates. Skippy was phenomenal and it was wonderful to see him perform. His famous "Flying Axel Paulsen" jump was a sight to open the eyes of all lovers of free skating. He seems to drift through the air rather than jump, and axels are as easy to him as ordinary "three jumps." Lidstone, the British champion five years in a row before the war, was no beginner to freestyle and knew of what he spoke.

Old Dreamland Rink

Baxter turned professional and skated in ice shows in the early 1940s. Because he was not interested in figures and seldom worked on them, he never did well in competitions, but he became a positive influence on the roller singles skaters in the 1940s. He convinced them that a good roller skater could jump as well as an ice skater. Baxter skated a demonstration on roller skates in New York, in 1940, doing a clean double salchow and ten consecutive axels, content not done by any roller skater before that time.

Heddy Stenuf, one of the leading ice skaters in the world, practiced her superb figures eight to ten hours a day and put in about one hour a day on freestyle. She was a gold test skater on ice and wished to pass all of her tests on rollers. Stenuf could also do the axel and double salchow jump on ice and rollers.

Stenauf and Baxter provided an inspiration to the roller skaters of the late 1930s and early 1940s. They encouraged the improvement of figure skating and free skating on rollers.

Another outstanding free skater of this period was Jack Seifert, 1943 champion. Gloria Nord, a very pretty roller skater, became a star in both movies and the Skating Vanities Roller Show, a traveling roller skating revue. Many amateurs joined the shows that formed in the 1940s. Nord encouraged ballet as part of every skater's training. Melva Block, noted as the best dressed skater in the 1940s, due to her skating wardrobe which cost thousands of dollars with some single outfits valued at two hundred dollars, a lot of money in those days. She was also a good figure and singles skater, capturing the Nationals in 1941 and 1942, the only woman to successfully defend her title in the first ten years of the RSROA Nationals. Margot Allred, who won in 1940, wore skates designed and patented by her father. The Allred skate became very popular during the 1940s. Shirley Snyder did the same thing with the Douglass-Snyder skate in 1943. Her father, Charles Snyder, a machinist from Dayton, Ohio, handmade her figure skates. These skates are now in the National Museum of Roller Skating's collection.

The content in singles remained basically the same as that of ice. Roller skaters do have a mechanical advantage when spinning, since there are four edges to use in combinations instead of just two that are popular on ice skates. There is also less friction, giving roller skaters an advantage in doing long combinations of jumps in a row.

A later development of roller skaters was the so called "traveling camel." (There has been some discussion among judges as to the validity of this name for this movement. Some ice skaters call it a "running camel.") This is a series of three turns in the arabesque (ballet position where your upper body and free leg are parallel to the floor) position, used to build up speed before setting the pivot of the spin. Introduced by Rick Mullican in 1958, it has since become a standard entrance into combination spins. Mullican actually used another technique, turning a rocker and a counter and maintaining an outside edge throughout the travel. Roller skaters invented the inverted camel position, introduced by Teddy Shufflebarger in 1946, though it did not become a popular item until much later, as many believed one had to be double jointed. Henry Haffke is also noted as doing this spin in the east. Most ice skaters still do not use this position while spinning. Sylvia Haffke introduced the heel camel, another roller skating innovation, in 1960. Sylvia was a leading contender in Senior Ladies Singles for the next ten years.

Gloria Nord

Margot Allred

After Skippy Baxter proved that axels and doubles done on ice skates could be done by a good roller skater, the proficiency of the jumpers improved. At first the jumps done on ice were the only ones tried on rollers. The single rotation flip, salchow, lutz, and loop were attempted. By 1946, the leading male roller skaters (J.W. Norcross, Jr., Clayton Doing, Norman Latin, and others) executed double jumps at the Nationals. It is interesting that the mapes jump, one of the more popular jumps today, came later. Ice skaters developed the jump as the "outside back toe loop." One of the leading ice skaters of the 1940s, Bruce Mapes, turned professional to skate in the ice shows. He used the "toe loop" often in his professional routines. The roller skaters picked this up and with the invention of better quality toe stop devices in 1946-1947, the "Mapes" jump became a more popular jump on rollers than on ice.

Some of the innovators in jumping were not always the champions. Alois Lutz presented the first lutz jump on ice skates in 1913. He was an Austrian ice skater who never was able to make that country's World Team. Bruce Towle did the first single lutz on rollers in 1940. He did this without any toe stops by touching the toe of his boot to the floor, but he did not win the competition.

Sylvia Haffke

In 1946, Norman Latin accomplished the first double lutz done in Nationals. Not a Senior that year, he won the Intermediate (Junior) division. The double loop jump was introduced by Jerry Nista in 1948. J. W. Norcross, Jr. executed the first double axel in National competition in 1950. Norcross won four Senior gold medals that year: Singles, Figures, Pairs, and Fours, a feat not yet been duplicated. Nancy Lee Parker became the first woman to do doubles (a salchow) in 1948. Ted Rosdahl also cleaned his double axel in 1951.

In 1953, Ron Ludington skated the first combination double axel-double loop in roller skating competition. Ludinton competed as a roller skater for many years. Today he is teaching ice skating and is one of the leading ice skating coaches in the United States. In 1959, only ten years after Dick Button astonished the world with the triple loop on ice, Gene Harless executed the first triples at the RSROA Nationals. Harless completed a clean triple mapes in 1959 and one year later he cleaned a triple toe walley. His jumping technique effortless, he jumped from a square position without turning into the jumps. In spite of his tremendous jumps, Harless did not even place in the event.

Laurene Anselmi reigned as the outstanding female skater of the 1950s. She won her first National titles in 1947, Juvenile Speed and Freestyle. She then won the Freestyle title in every event she entered, including Senior Ladies, over the next eight years. She was also a National Champion in Figures, Pairs, and Fours skating.

Bruce Towle

Even though numerous skaters did triples in the 1950's and 1960s, few doubt that Michael Jacques put the triple jumps into every

Senior man's repertoire. Jacques dominated the RSROA Senior Men's event winning seven consecutive times (1966-1972). When Jacques began in Senior Men, only the top few men were able to do a triple jump. By the time he retired, almost every finalist attempted a triple with confidence. Double axel and double boeckl jumps were done by the women and young skaters. Jacques was so consistent he could do triples in combination with other very difficult jumps. Jacques and Scott Harrity, from Pontiac, Michigan, were the first to do the triple OB (outside back) loop at the Nationals in 1969. Rick Ellsworth and Tim McGuire did a triple lutz and triple flip at Nationals in the 1980s.

Until 1949, Figure Skating Champions performed both Figures and Freestyle skating combined. In 1949, individual champions were declared, although Figures remained used to select the Freestyle contestants. Later this requirement was also dropped and the singles skaters did their routine for both eliminations and finals.

The scores that a skater received in the elimination round added to the scores received in the final until 1948. After 1948, each was considered as a separate and new contest, with the lower placed skater in the eliminations not at such an extreme disadvantage in the final.

The increase in content levels was greater after the separation of Figures and Singles, but the level of proficiency in skating movements somewhat declined. RSROA American skaters of the 1950s were noted for their tremendous content and poor programs as compared to the International skaters. However, in the 1960s and 1970s, several young skaters with good style and content began to emerge. Ellen Meade from Florida and April Allen from Texas showed that good content goes with good footwork, music, and ballet movements. In the 1970s people compared Allen to the great ice stars because of her fantastic routines. Daryl Bayles, a leading contender in Senior Men Singles, skated very interpretative routines with strong content, including a double axel and two triples in 1971. Scott Cohen demonstrated superior style and interpretation, along with difficult content, winning several National and World Titles in Singles in the 1990s. Cohen presented a short program to a tango in 1993 that brought audiences to their feet, tears of joy in their eyes, a routine considered by many to be among the most outstanding freestyle programs of all time.

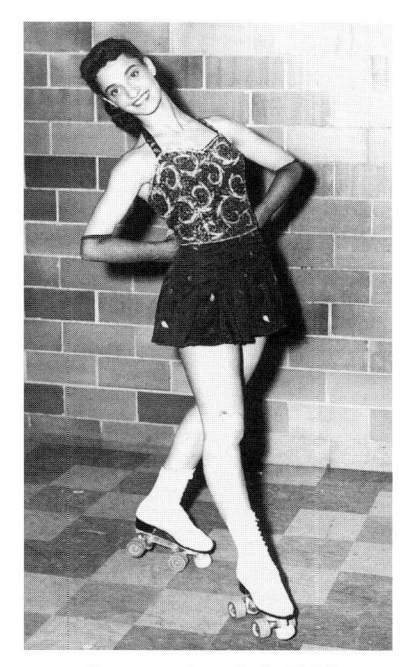

Laurene Anselmi, 1950

Michael Jacques

8 PAIRS AND FOURS SKATING

Nancy Kromis, Richard McLauchlen, John Matejec

Pairs skating as we know it developed from ballet movements. Lifts, arabesques, and shadow movements all found in ballet were put into a couples routine and performed to music.

Pairs skating was included in the first artistic roller championship in 1939. Eldora Andrews and Bill Best won the championship that year. Content levels at this time were very low and the routines consisted mostly of shadow footwork, simple waist and underarm lifts, and upright pair spins. Though some pairs skated in vaudeville in the 1920s, but their performance consisted mostly of "flying" and "swing the lady around" tricks, not really artistic or ballet oriented movements.

One of the first pairs innovators was pro Bill McMillan, who invented the "pass-over axel" in 1943. The team of Bill Martin and Margret Williams, McMillan's team skating from Detroit, won the championship that year. This team also executed the first pairs OB (outside back) camels in 1943.

After the improvements of toe stops in 1946, the spike toe off lifts became popular, especially the split lutz lift. The common practice was that a team could not do a pairs lift if it was a jump that a woman could not perform by herself. For example, a lutz lift in stag position, rotating four times around was not acceptable, since this would be an impossible thing for the woman to do without the man's assistance. Judges learned to look for continuous up and down movement in a lift. Teams did not jump, lock into a press position, rotate, and then exit, as is the common practice today. This would be called a "carry lift," no credit was given, and points were often deducted from the manner of performance score.

Bill Martin & Margaret Williams, 1942

The first contact pairs jump was the contact single salchow accomplished in 1948 by Ada Duerlein and Donald Craig from Pittsburgh, Pennsylvania. Contact jumps became a required piece of content in the 1950s. Contact one and a half rotation jumps then developed, and the better teams in the 1960s did the contact boeckl and axel. No one has yet executed a contact double jump (with both partners doing a double). While theoretically possible, the complications of the double rotation in contact are quite formidable. Most teams do the double as an underarm move, the woman turning the double under the man's arm, or as a throw jump. In 1972, the contact jump requirement was removed with the recent trend to reduce the importance of these items. Contact jumps were not included in European pairs routines until recently.

Cecil Davis and Phyllis Bulleigh, the Pairs champions in 1948, 1949, and 1951, developed the first layback pairs spins. The man does a regular camel with the woman doing an inverted camel beside or directly below him. This led to the "Impossible Spin," so named because the woman could not execute the item solo, as she is suspended in mid-air below the man's camel spin. It

Cecil Davis & Phyllis Bulleigh, 1952

was introduced in 1956 by Warren Colozzo and Patricia Benedict as they gained a second Senior Pairs title in the RSROA Nationals.

Through the years there have been many fine pairs teams. In the mid 1960s, David Tassinari invented a spin in which just as his partner, Diane Kearns, pulled into the OB pairs camel, he would leap over her back and, landing on the other side, do the pairs camel. This exciting and novel "jump outside back" pairs camel or "The Tassinari Camel" was a real crowd pleaser and added greatly to Tassinari and Kearn's routine.

Ron and Gail Robovitsky from Michigan dominated the pairs event in the latter 1960's. U.S. champions from 1967 to 1972 and World Champions from 1970 to 1972, they executed lifts as difficult and as well as the Russian Olympic Champions on ice in that era. They introduced full extension lifts, one hand lifts, and complicated combination lifts to roller pairs. Their spins were excellent too, and they introduced the "impossible" traveling camel-- the man does a traveling camel with the lady suspended in the air, in a one arm grip, underneath him.

David Tassinari & Diane Kearns

The Robovitsky's were always excellent in their strength items, with exciting though not always balletic performances. After their retirement, the successors in Senior Pairs, Ray Chappata and Karen Mejia were the ultimate in artistic pairs. Both of these skaters trained in ballet and attended an advanced ballet academy as well as skating in World competition. Their artistic style has remained unmatched and their skating coach, Tim Able, encouraged them to incorporate ballet type training in their pairs routine. This helped them to win U.S. Championship and World titles.

These two teams have left a legacy to the future pairs teams. The Robovitsky's strength and the Chappata-Mejia artistic impression have inspired the American coaches and skaters.

FOURS

The Fours Skating Event grew out of combination figure skating on ice in the 1920s. The team was composed of two pairs teams, required to execute Singles, Pairs, and Fours movements during the routine. The champion Fours teams were usually composed of outstanding Pairs teams, but many skaters formed Fours teams to bring along a weaker skater or weaker team still developing as Single or Pairs skaters.

The first Fours event was skated in the RSROA Nationals in 1942. Dorothy Law, Louise Moore, Bill Martin, and Alden Sibley, from Detroit won the first championship. Martin developed as a Senior Pairs champion the next year with a

Ron & Gale Robovitsky

different partner, Margaret Williams. Bill McMillan became the pro of this Fours team and one of the innovators in the event of Fours skating.

Numerous great all around skaters also did well in Pairs and Fours in the first ten years of the event. Looking through the list of Fours team champions brings up great skating names like Pat Carroll, Norman Latin, J. W. Norcross, Robert Labriola, Nancy Kromis, John Matejec, William Pate, Ron Jellse, and others.

In 1952, a Fours team from Middleton, Ohio, won the Intermediate Division and are credited with the invention of the "fours pendulum swing spin" that year. This became a standard item in every team's repertoire. Frances Recher, Gary Houck, Maxine Dorn, and Billy Stricklen made the "Fabulous Fours" their nickname. In 1954, Recher and Houck teamed up with another pair, Robert Clary and Marilee Olson, and captured the Senior Fours crown.

Chuck Little, Dorothy Law, Doug Breniser & Louise Moore, 1946

From 1963 to 1974, California dominated the Fours event, usually placing two of the three top teams in Seniors. The leading coaches in this form of skating, Tom Panno and James Pringle, showed over a twelve year period superior knowledge and innovation in Fours skating.

Richard Toon skated in more Senior Fours champion teams than any other person (six times). Judy Jerue and Dennis Collier are equally familiar names on the winners platform. Louis Stovall and the team from Long Beach in 1972 broke the domination of the San Leandro teams who won five years consecutively. Stovall went on to skate and win the Senior Pairs World title in 1973, after placing second in the United States championships with Vicky Handyside.

Although the Fours events were not as large a competitive field as other events (being reduced to only two divisions in 1967), the best teams were composed of some of the best Pairs and Singles skaters at that time.

There are many problems in developing a Fours team including deciding on a practice schedule, finding four people with compatible personalities, and with close levels of proficiency. In 1974, USAC dropped Fours events at the Nationals due to lack of participation. However, Fours are still done at the Gold Skate Classic, shows, and exhibitions.

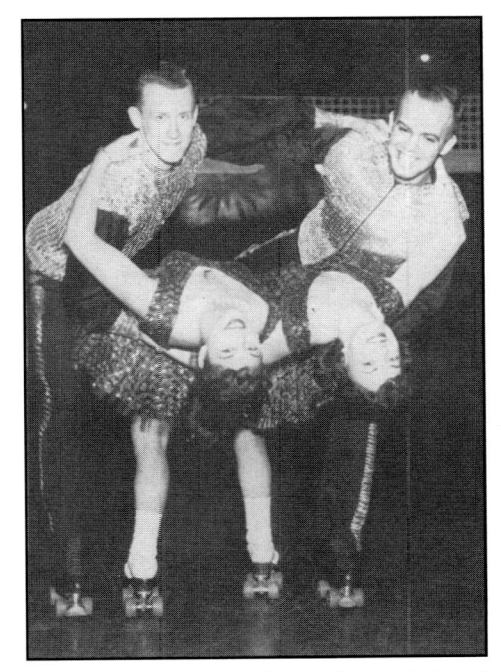

Ron Jellse, Ruth Ann Koch, Carol Haller & Bob Anderson, 1956

9 SPEED

Fred "Bright Star" Muree, 1939

As soon as men put on skates, he wanted to see how fast he could go. Speed skating and racing have been one of the oldest forms of skating, ice or roller.

During the boom period of the 1880s, one of the most interesting speed skaters was Fred Muree, also known as "Bright Star," a Native American born in 1861 in a little village near Omaha, Nebraska. Around that time, the government rounded up the Native Americans living in that area and moved them to a reservation in Oklahoma. Muree's father knew that life on the reservation would not be good for his family, so he loaded up a pony cart and they walked to Boston, Massachusetts. Muree, 16 years old, began to attend school.

Muree got a job in a Boston roller rink as a "skate boy," the one who helped patrons put on their skates. Rinks were frequently operated by a skate company. Plimpton, American Club Skates, Nuit Skate Company, Martha's Vineyard Skates by Winslow, Hygenic Skates, Richardson Skates, Raymond, and Union Hardware all operated rinks in the 1880s.

Muree worked for the Plimpton Skate Rink in 1880 and Professor Agerton, a coach and a friend of J. L. Plimpton, gave him a pair of speed skates with pin bearing wheels, ball bearings were not used at the time. In the early days competent instructors were called "Professors," which later became "professionals." Muree, with his new skates, learned the sport while working at the rink. After Muree worked for the rink eight months, a five mile race open to skaters under 18 years old was announced.

Muree began training for the race. Eighteen entrants started but only three finished. The favorite was Kenneth Skinner, the fastest speed skater at that time in the Boston area, with a record 16 minutes for five miles. However, Muree won the race with a 15.52 - eight seconds faster than Skinner's previous record.

When the story of Muree's win hit the newspapers, Frank Clayton, manager of the Argyle Rink in Boston signed Fred to a contract to race for his rink. Fred's father was to receive $1,000 when Fred reached age 21. During 1880-1881 Fred skated in 284 five-mile races for Clayton, winning them all!

Fred Muree was not happy with the terms of his contract. He ran away from Clayton, but later returned on a salary of $100.00 per week plus expenses. He finished out his contract but his father was never paid the $1000 indenture owed to him by Clayton. After he was 21, Muree raced professionally winning about 50% of his starts.

Kenneth Skinner introduced the first ball bearing speed skate. Muree received the second pair made. In his next race, he skated five miles on the same track where he set his first record in 15 minutes flat. A professional race this time and he won against Skinner again.

In 1881 the first six-day marathon race was held at the old Madison Square Gardens in New York City. Mr. Donovan, the fastest pro-racer in the 1870s, won the race. Three weeks later, he died of pneumonia brought on by the strain of the race. Following Donovan's death, New York City passed an ordinance limiting racing to 144 hours per week.

The next big endurance race occurred in 1882, a 72-hour race, the legal limit for continuous skating in New York. Fred Muree was not entered in this race. Fred Snowton of Boston won, Charlie Walton came in second, Jimmy Omelia third, and Eugene Maddox fourth. Conditions were improving so much with the use of ball bearing wheels that the skaters covered 1,124 miles in the 72 hours. In the past that distance would have taken 144 hours on old model skates without ball bearings.

The skating boom in 1880 began to decline with the decline in the economy. Skating rinks, theaters, and dance halls all suffered with many closing the doors. In 1887 very few rinks existed outside of Chicago. The interest in roller skating, though declining in America, still flourished in Europe in the 1890s. The Raymond Skate Company sent Muree to skate in Australia, but when he got to England he decided to tour Europe instead. He raced in Italy, Germany, France, and other European countries clearing $10,000 before returning home. Fred Muree, "Bright Star," gave exhibitions and managed rinks all over the U.S. He died in 1950 after a full life of roller skating.

Harley Davidson became the next great speed skater following Fred Muree. Though not associated with Harley-Davidson motorcycles, he often told people such for publicity purposes. Born in 1881, he came from a family of skaters. Harley's father, John X. Davidson, was noted as one of the best skaters in Ohio in the 1870s. Harley's family moved to St. Paul, Minnesota, where the children all learned to ice skate on Lake Como. They were all good roller skaters, too. Harley first roller skated in 1884 at the age of three. His family later toured Europe giving exhibitions on ice and roller skating.

Harley Davidson

Harley Davidson first started competitive skating around 1892. He defeated Joseph F. Donohugue of New York in ice speed skating on the Hudson River. He became the American Ice Speed Skating Champion setting several records on ice skates. In 1904 Harley returned to roller skating, and in 1905 began to race professionally on rollers. It is for his accomplishments as a roller skater that he is best remembered.

One of the most memorable races was the 1909 World Professional Championships held at the Olympia Rink in London, England. The competition began with 150 skaters. The field narrowed down to five finalists: Harley, his bother John Davidson, Allie Moore from Michigan, and C.J. Wilson and P.F. Powell, both from England. 14,000 spectators watched the finals. The track at the Olympia Rink was massive for its time. Free of obstructions of any kind, the track was six laps, five hundred and sixty feet to the mile (16 laps per mile is a normal rink track today). The great length and width of the skating surface, along with a large seating capacity on the main floor and balcony, made the Olympia Rink an excellent place to hold a World Championship race. The finals were skated on February 26, 1909. Harley Davidson won followed by Allie Moore, C.J. Wilson, John Davidson and finally P.F. Powell. Harley received a diamond studded medal and a first prize purse of $2000 in gold.

Over the next three years (1909-1911), Harley Davidson raced in America, Canada, and Europe against the best speed skaters of his time in challenge matches. He was usually victorious against such great skaters as Fred Martin, Arthur Eglington, Roland Cioni, Frank Bacon, Rodney Peters, and Jesse Carey. He also established the Harley Davidson Professional Speed Skating Troupe in 1911. This group of professional racers toured the U.S. giving skating and racing exhibitions.

In 1911 at the St. Louis Jai Alai Arena, Harley skated in the two-mile Professional Championship. Most of the great speed skaters of the day entered including Lawrence Sibenaler, 1910 Oklahoma State Champion, Rodney Peters, the St. Louis Champion and World Champion, McKinley of Chicago, G. Edwards and G. Peters of St. Louis, Jack Fotch of Michigan, Harley Davidson, Fred Martin, the 1910 Pacific Coast Champion, Fred Tyrell of Chicago, the 1909 Illinois State Champion, "Midge" Sherman, Louis Bradbury of Kansas City, Jesse Carey, the European and World Amateur Champion, Roland Cioni, World Professional Champion 1914-1921, Frank Bacon, the "Billboard" Champion, and Ray O'Neil, St. Louis City Champion 1910-1916.

Jesse Carey

Harley Davidson gradually retired from roller speed skating beginning in 1916 switching to performing fancy skating and dance exhibitions. He did not have a rink managing job to fall back like many speed skaters, and times often proved hard for him financially. His former competitors credited him as the greatest racer of his time. Harley Davidson started in over 4,000 races and won 3,035, plus many seconds and thirds. He won over 200 medals along with silver cups, trophies, awards, and plaques. He also set six World Speed Skating records.

Fred Martin, from Los Angles, California, reigned as the Professional Speed Champion of the Pacific Coast until 1910. He then went east and skated in a professional meet at the Wayne Rink in Detroit. Martin met Joseph Munch, the Northwest Champion (actually the Great Lakes States) and they began training and skating as a team. The pair entered a 24-hour race at the Riverview Rink in Milwaukee, Wisconsin, which Martin won. He covered 253 miles and 12 laps setting a new World's record. Martin stayed in the Midwest winning many races in Milwaukee and Chicago from 1914 to 1915.

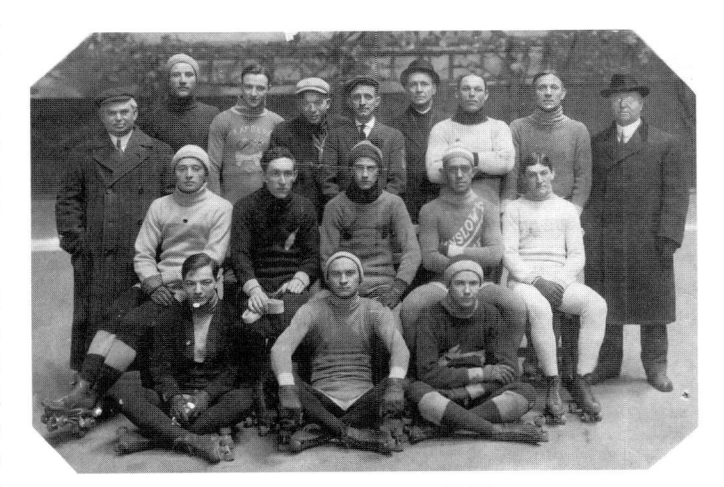

Speed Skaters, Early 1900's

Fred Martin, 1912

Martin then teamed up with Frank Bacon and entered the 24 hour team race at the Convention Hall Rink in Washington, D.C. in March, 1915. They placed second to the World Champion team of Roland Cioni and Arthur Eglington. Martin and Bacon again placed second to Cioni and Eglington in the 100 Mile American Derby that year.

Fred Martin returned to Milwaukee and became the floor manager of the Riverview Rink. People knew him as a good rink manager, and he later managed rinks in Chicago and Michigan. He helped to found the RSROA in 1937 while he was the manager of the Arena Gardens in Detroit.

Rodney R. Peters, another great speed skater from 1907 to 1922, he started skating at the Crescent Rink in St. Louis, Missouri. He competed in the first World Amateur Championships in 1908 held at the Jai Alai Rink in St. Louis. Also in 1908, he won the prestigious Harmon Cup at the World Championships held at the Riverview Rink in Chicago.

Peters then began an extensive tour of the U.S., skating challenge races against anyone and everyone. During this tour he won and defended the one mile championship in Pittsburgh and established a flat track World record of two minutes, 46.4 seconds.

Toward the end of 1909, Peters traveled to Europe to skate in international races being held. In a meet held at the Earl's Court Rink in London, England, he defeated Allie Moore, one of the world's best racers, and Charles Wilson, the champion of England at that time. Peters won every race he entered in 1910 in both England and France. In 1911, he returned to the U.S. to compete in the championship races in St. Louis that year.

Starting in 1912, Peters began to manage roller rinks in the St. Louis area; Delmar Gardens in 1912, San Soucci in 1913, and the Palladium in 1914. Rodney still remained active in racing all around the country. In 1916 he entered the World Championships, setting a new record for the one mile. Because of the first World War, as well as for business reasons, Peters retired from racing in 1917. His retirement lasted only three years, for in 1921 Peters returned to skating. He skated a two mile race at the Palladium Rink, establishing a new record of five minutes, 48 seconds. Peters also entered the Leo Seltzer Roller Derby in 1935. He coached many speed skaters including the first U.S. Speed Champion (RSROA), Lloyd "Whitey" Christopher, in 1937. He was one of the 17 founding fathers of the RSROA along with Fred Martin, Vic Brown, and Al Kish.

Lloyd "Whitey" Christopher, First RSROA Speed Skating Champion, 1937

Though relatively few skaters today have heard of Roland Cioni, those who do remember him as a coach of artistic skating whose pupils nearly dominated the National Championships in the 1940s and early 1950s. Before his career as a coach, however, Cioni reigned as the number one ranked professional skater in the world from 1913 to 1917. Cioni was "Mr. Speed," acknowledged by many as one of the greatest, if not the greatest, roller speed skater the sport has ever known.

Roland Cioni born in Norristown, Pennsylvania, in 1896, started skating in amateur speed competitions at the age of six. In a few years he became the talk of the skating world in speed sprint racing. In 1910, Roland joined the Professional speed skating circuit, and although he didn't win every race, he finished consistently high, gaining a reputation as one of best new skaters in professional racing.

Cioni became an original member of Harley Davidson's Professional Speed Skating Troupe, which was organized in St. Louis, Missouri in January of 1911. The tour of this group, known as "Harley Davidson's World Champions," began in February of that year and covered all 48 United States. Along with racing between the members of the troupe, these speed skaters challenged all comers from the local towns in exhibition races. Together with Cioni and the others previously mentioned, the group included: Fred Tyrell, Louis Sibenolar, and Jack Fotch.

In 1912, the Davidson Speed Skating Troupe dissolved with each of the racers went their own way. For Cioni, it was just the beginning of an illustrious career. In addition to sprint match races, Cioni started to skate in the endurance or marathon races, just then becoming popular in the United States. He soon showed he had staying power in addition to speed. In a 24 hour marathon contest held in March of 1913 at Milwaukee's Riverview Rink, he placed second to Fred Martin in the race.

One year later, on March 25,1914, Roland Cioni won his first World Professional Speed Skating Championship at the Palace Rink in Detroit. During 1915, Cioni successfully defended his title against the best speed skaters in the country, including Fred Martin and Jesse Carey. Cioni's picture soon appeared in newspapers throughout the world. Crowds packed Madison Square Garden in New York and every other important racing center following announcement that he would be competing. In April of 1916, Cioni again defeated all his competitors and retained the World Professional Speed Racing title for a third consecutive year, the first time any racer accomplished this feat. In 1916, Cioni was actually co-champion at the World meet held at the Riverview Rink in Chicago. Cioni's partner in the team competition, Arthur Eglington of England, tied Cioni in total points that time. The overall champion was determined by points scored. For each race, points were awarded for placing first though fifth and then the total points added together to determine the World Champion. For the next five years, Cioni continued to dominate the professional circuit, winning additional World titles from 1917 to 1921.

Roland Cioni, 1921

After 1914, when he first won the World title, Roland Cioni remained undefeated in individual competition until his retirement, in 1921, after capturing eight straight World Roller Speed Racing titles.

Cioni teamed up with Arthur Eglington to form one of the fastest and most durable relay teams of the professional era. In 1915 and 1916, the duo consistently won endurance races, setting many distance records. While skating alone, Cioni set a record in the 100 mile timed marathon on a flat track in Washington, D.C.

Along with his talents on the track, Cioni was quite knowledgeable about rink operations. He became a rink manager in September, 1916, when Chicago's Dreamland Rink first opened, and began teaching skating in 1919. With his wife Margaret, Cioni became a full time skating instructor in 1936, teaching in Hackensack, New Jersey, and White Plains, New York. He joined the staff of the Park Circle Rink in Brooklyn, NY, in 1942. The Cioni's turned out National Champions by the dozens until their retirement. Roland Cioni passed away in September, 1959. He was posthumously elected to USAC/RS' Coaches Hall of Fame in 1991.

1916 Professional Speed Skaters

Many others became interesting speed skating personalities in these early years. Walter Osmun was racing professionally at the turn of the century as an endurance racer in 1885, and skated a ten-hour race covering 136.5 miles in Fond du Lac, Wisconsin. He also established a record of 780 miles in a 72-hour marathon (skating 12 hours a day for six days) in Minneapolis, Minnesota. These records lasted for 30 years. Walter was also known for "one foot racing"— skating on his right foot gaining momentum with his left. His one foot records were as fast as some two skate records. He remained active in Michigan until the 1920s as a rink manager and officer in the Western Skating Association.

Joseph W. Munch reigned as the Western Skating Association (regional skating association in the midwest at the turn of the century) champion speed skater from 1905-1912. One championship title was a diamond studded gold medal won in Milwaukee in December 1909. He entered amateur and then pro races (1908-1913) until he lost his title to Frank Bryant of Duluth, Minnesota in February 1913. Following this defeat, he managed rinks and coached Allie Moore and Fred Martin during their racing careers at the Riverview Rink in Milwaukee, Wisconsin.

Silver medals given for speed skating, 1885.

Frank Bryant was the Northwestern Professional Champion (Western Skating Association) from 1913-1916. Born in Detroit, Michigan in 1887, he began skating in Duluth, Minnesota in 1901. His first professional race was for the Great Lakes Championship. He defeated Ed Moe, the reigning champion, in three races of one, two, and three miles. Bryant defeated Munch and won the Northwestern Professional Championship in 1913. He won four of five races, setting the track record of two minutes, 49 seconds in the mile. Bryant held the title for the next three years. During his career, Frank Bryant won 211 races, loosing only 19.

Leon Kimm, an outstanding amateur skater in the early twentieth century, from Chicago won the World Amateur Title from 1912-1914. From 1908-1914 he placed first, second, or third in all international competitions that he entered. He also trained with Carl Carlson to win the U.S. Relay Team Title from 1912-1913, skating for the Western Skating Association. Kimm helped to uphold amateur roller sports in an era of professional racing.

Bill Henning was born March 15, 1890 in Chicago. He began as a skate boy in 1908 at the Riverview Rink in Chicago, a speed skating center at that time with Fred Martin, Harley Davidson, and Jesse Carey skating there from 1914 to 1915. Henning began skating in amateur races, but in 1916 he moved to pro racing. Henning joined the Navy and was named Roller Skating Champion of the South Atlantic Fleet, based in Philadelphia, in 1919. In 1922, after his discharge from the Navy, Henning went to Baltimore, Maryland and managed Carlin's Roller Rink. In 1923 he won a 21-day World Championship meet for Professionals held in Baltimore. In 1928 he became Maryland State Champion and in 1929 he raced from Washington D.C. to Baltimore on a highway. Out of the 76 entrants in the race, Henning was the oldest. He finished third with a time of five hours and fifteen minutes for 51 miles covered. Later in 1929, Henning entered the World Championship Race at the Chicago Stadium. The event lasted 21 days but Henning had to withdraw after a few days due to injury.

Bill Henning, 1931

At the age of 40, in 1931, Bill Henning began a cross country trip from Baltimore to San Diego. A support car carrying spare skate parts, 12 pairs of skate boots, and 200 sets of rubber and metal wheels followed him. His route went through New Orleans and along the Old Spanish Trail through Louisiana, Texas, and New Mexico to the west coast. Henning reached San Diego in 69 days, having used up five pairs of boots and 127 sets of wheels.

Throughout the 1930s Henning remained a devoted speed skater, hockey promoter, and then joined the Transcontinental Roller Derby in 1935. He managed rinks in the Chicago area until 1940 and remained active in skating through the Old Timers Club in Chicago.

At first (1880-1940) skaters used the loose ball bearings. In the 1940s, artistic skaters introduced precision bearings, but most speed skaters stayed with the loose ball type. In the l950s speed skaters continued to feel that a faster roll was accomplished with loose ball bearings. However, in the 1970s speed skaters renewed their interest in the precision bearing using a very light oil in speed wheels. (Another technique is to use self-locking axle nuts which do not put undue side pressure on the bearings.) Manufacturers introduced lighter skate plates with holes drilled out of them or molded from light weight plastic or metal which maintains the strength of the plate but lessens the weight.

Skaters from the Transcontinental Roller Derby, 1935

In speed skating a lot of credit should go to the officials and National

Speed Committees that govern this branch of the sport. The speed representatives constantly try out new systems and innovations to improve their sport. These representatives, more than any single champion, have done much to bring speed skating to its present point of development.

Very few "perennial" speed champions are able to win the Senior event year after year. The competition is very keen, the top skaters are too close each year to allow a single skater to dominate unchallenged. In the early years of speed competition, only the Senior events existed. However, as more skaters entered competition, lower qualifying events were added by age group with the mixed and four person relay races added later.

A lot of roller skating in the 1920s occurred outdoors. There was Frank Klopp from Philadelphia who set the World amateur record of 2:45.6 for the one mile outdoors, on August 2, 1921. The previous mile of 2:51.4 had held since 1901. Endurance skating was also popular. In May 1923, Leo Harman skated 50 hours straight. Walter Miller in June, 1935 performed the longest marathon. He skated 147 hours, with a few rest periods, at the White City Rink in Boise, Idaho.

Speed skating was especially popular in Chicago and New York City. In New York, the City Recreation Department sponsored Roller Skating Speed tournaments starting in 1925 held on concrete surfaces in New York's Central Park. As many as 8,000 children and adults raced in the qualifying heats at various city playgrounds. Races ranged from the 100 yard dash to the 880 yard race. Victors won a pair of skates. This became an annual event in New York.

Road touring, still very popular in Europe, was more common in America in the twenties. In 1927, Mrs. Henry Pfetzing and her daughter, Anna Catherine, skated from Kansas City, Missouri to Peoria, Illinois, a distance of 400 miles. They skated as much of the distance as possible, but due to dirt roads and uncooperative local officials that would not allow them to skate through certain towns, they only covered 215 miles on skates.

Arthur Allegretti skated from Buffalo, New York to New York City in 1927, to win a bet with a friend. On Tuesday, August 9, he left Buffalo with a letter signed by the Mayor of that city, Mr. Schwab. Allegretti skated for 58 hours with no sleep. He carried no food but stopped at hot dog stands along the road, substituting for the entire trip on a diet of hot dogs and grape pop, as well as other occasional snacks. Arthur arrived in New York City on Thursday, August 11, in the evening and skated to City Hall only to find that the Mayor of New York City out of town. He decided to check in at the nearby Police Station and related the story to one of "New York's Finest" for verification of his arrival and completed his journey in order to win his wager.

In 1929, one of the premier races of this era was a six day marathon to be skated non-stop by three man teams from June 11 to June 16,

1913 Woman Speed Skater

1929 held at Madison Square Garden in New York City. The roster of contestants consisted of a regular "who's who" of international speed skating. Arthur Eglington, from Great Britain held every British speed record, and entered on a team with two Americans, one of whom, Joe West was the Amateur Champion of the world. Leo Coltrona came from Italy where he reigned as Italian National Speed Champion to skate in the event. Joey Ray, the great middle distance runner from Chicago, donned skates for the race. Al Kish, who later helped found the RSROA, led a team from Cleveland, Ohio.

The rules were the same basic ones as used in the bicycle "grinds" popular at this time. One man per team raced while his mates rested in bunks set up along side the track. Sprint periods were held at 3:00 p.m., 9:00 p.m., and 2:00 a.m., and the teams must go all out during these times, no pacing allowed. Sixteen teams entered the event.

At the end of the first evening of racing, the British-American team of Eglington, West, and Woodruff stood first; the Italian-American team of Coltrona, Howard, and Murray second; and third was the Brooklyn team of Gorman, Gregory, and Ryder. The leaders covered a distance of 10 miles in the first 1/2 hour of racing. However, this rapid pace could not be maintained for very long if the teams intended to last the entire six days.

On the second day, Al Kish's team from Cleveland moved into the lead. Joey Ray's team from Chicago overtook Kish's for a short time, but the Cleveland team held the lead at the end of the night. By the finish of the second day, three teams withdrew from the race.

On the third day of racing, Ray's Chicago team won the lead as the British-American team was forced to withdraw. Judges, however, allowed Eglington to join the Brooklyn team to replace Murry Gorman who could not continue. A team from the "Twin Cities," Harley Davidson, Everett McGowan, and William Ordson took over second place. The "new" Brooklyn team held third.

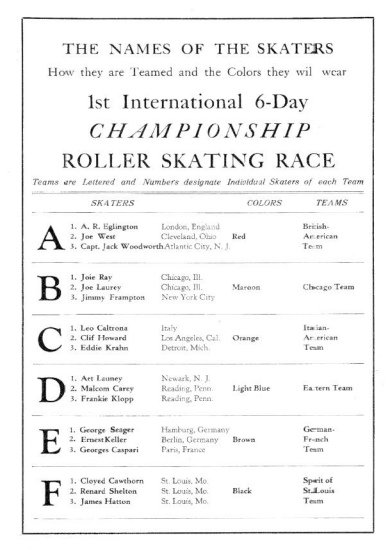

Official program of the 1st International 6-day Roller Skating Championship, 1929

By June 14, only eight of the starting sixteen teams remained in the race. The Chicago team still held first, the Brooklyn team second, three miles behind, and the Cleveland team a close third.

The Ray team from Chicago was forced to retire from the race on the last day. Only five teams finished the race, and the results were as follows:

1. Eglington - Gillespie - Ryder	1246 Miles, 8 laps
2. Kish - Thomas - Bradic	1245 Miles, 4 laps
3. Davidson - McGowan - Dodson	1239 Miles, 9 laps
4. Cawthorn - Shelton - Hatton	1227 Miles, 5 laps
5. Launey - Carey - Krahn	1226 Miles, 0 laps

The well-publicized race brought out large crowds of spectators several nights.

Other marathon endurance races of this kind took place over the next several years. Notable was the 1932 twenty-one day race sponsored by Vic Brown and the Dreamland Rink in Newark, NJ. After 19 days of relay team racing judges declared the race over, due to snow on the outdoor track. Bob Ringwald, Claude Hawthorne, and Midge Reiff were declared the winners.

In 1936, an Amateur International meet was held, sponsored by the Federation Internationale de Patinage Roulette's (now the Federation Internationale de Roller Skating, FIRS). Speed and hockey events were staged at the Stadthall Sports Arena in Germany, which would hold 10,000 spectators.

The speed track was only three meters wide, under ten feet. Skaters from Great Britain, France, Germany, Switzerland, Belgium, Portugal, and Italy entered. Britain and France with the fastest skaters, won most of the placements. The U.S. skaters did not compete because there was not a U.S. National Skating Association in 1936, like the NSA of Great Britain, to join FIRS.

In 1935, entrepreneur, Leo A. Seltzer formed the Transcontinental Roller Derby in a Chicago restaurant. He was looking for a sport with thrills and excitement to fill the Chicago Coliseum. Seltzer and friends dining with him, brainstormed ideas until they came up with "roller speed skating on a banked bicycle track." The early rules resembled those of six-day bicycle races, popular in that era. Diners drew the diagram of the track and rules on the restaurant tablecloth.

Al Kish, 1927

The original roller derby differed some what from the later forms of the game. The object of the derby was to skate the distance between Chicago and San Francisco or New York and San Diego - two cities at least half a continent apart - in the quickest time. Two teams participated in the race on a banked track with laps per mile figured and marked as completed. A team consisted of 10 active male and female skaters. Each team skated for 15 minutes, boys and girls alternating. Teams earned points by passing a member of a rival team by circling the track and passing from the rear. The team with the most points after the allotted mileage won. Some races lasted as long as 24 hours. Winners received prize money. Often amateurs and professionals raced against each other. Some special events pitted local stars against a traveling roller derby team. Roller derby was filmed and televised and it was one of the most popular shows on television in the 1950s.

The first official U.S. Amateur Speed Skating Championship races were held at the Arena Gardens Roller Skating Rink in Detroit, Michigan, from April 2nd through 4th, 1937. The races were sponsored by the Michigan Skating Association and sanctioned by the Amateur Skating Union of the United States. Twenty-three competitors entered in the Senior Men's division to crown a champion. At the same time, the Inter-City Woman's Amateur Speed Skating Championships were held. Most of the competitors in 1937 came from Detroit. Other cities represented included Chicago, Cleveland,

Cincinnati, St. Louis, and from the east coast, Boston and Newark.

Men won the championship on the basis of overall point standings from the five different events held: the 440 and 880 yard, and the one, two, and five mile races. Points were awarded only for the placement in the finals of each event: 30 for 1st, 20 for 2nd, and 10 points for 3rd place. Lloyd Christopher of the Palladium Rink, in St. Louis, became the overall men's champion, with a total of 100 points. Christopher won the two and five mile events, and placed 2nd in both the 440 and 880 yard races. Edward Theiner (of the 100 Club) in Detroit, finished second overall with 60 points. Theiner won the 880 yard, took second in the two mile and third in the five mile race. The winner of the 440 yard event was Vincent Vassali of the Dreamland Rink in Newark. Norman McGinnis, also from the 100 club in Detroit, captured the one mile race. Other skaters entered in the competition included Harry Schierbaum, Harold Saindon, and Edward Chudy of Chicago; Austin Thorton, Erving Reznick, Don Hamel, Leonard Godfrey, Armand Johnson and Dudley Maher of Detroit; Louis Bick of Newmark; Ernest and John Scott, Jr. of Boston; Frank Wermes, Arthur and Bert Emanual, Hershel Rhodes, Joe Ketter and John Uebel, all from Ohio; and Kenneth Haller of Pittsburgh, PA.

As with the men's competition, the overall champion of the 1937 Inter-City Women's meet was determined by a points system based on three different events held. Nancy Flick of the Rollerdrome from Cincinnati emerged the winner. Flick took first in the 440 yard and one mile races, capturing the overall title with 60 points. Vivian Bell, also from Rollerdrome, placed second overall with 40 points from her second place finishes in both the 880 yard and one mile events. Bell became the first Women's Champion (RSROA) in 1938. The winner of the 880 yard race, Verna Picton of the Arena Gardens of Detroit, finished in a tie overall with Virginia Hancock of Detroit. Picton eventually captured the U.S. Women's title in 1940. Other competitors in the 1937 Inter-City meet included LaVeta Deemer, Shirley Hill, Beatrice Hancock, Helen Fleece, Helen and Mary Cunniff, and Ann Manion of Detroit; Mary Lou Clark of Cincinnati; Caroline Marquardt of St. Louis; Lillian Lewis of Cleveland; and Virginia Schwartz of Navarre, Ohio.

Great skaters in speed for the 1940s and 1950s included many fine athletes. Pro racing was not popular at this time, and the RSROA and USARSA sought to develop amateur skating as part of the sport of roller skating. After WWII, the sport grew and with the developments of the RSROA as a governing body for amateur skaters, both speed and

Roller Derby, 1950

Arena Gardens Roller Rink, Detroit, Mich.

Vivian Bell (left), 1938 RSROA Speed Champion

artistic skating flourished.

One of the outstanding speed skaters of the 1950s was Charles Wahlig. Wahlig also was an outstanding artistic skater as he won Nationals in both dance and speed. In 1957, Wahlig won the Senior Dance and Senior Men's Speed titles, the first person to win National Senior titles in two disciplines (artistic & speed) during the same year. He became the first person to pass both Dance and Speed Skating Gold medal tests, accomplishing this feat in 1953. Wahlig won the Senior Dance title again in 1958 and 1959, and also captured the World Roller Skating Congress Dance title in 1959. From 1953 through 1960, Wahlig placed either first or second in National Senior Dance competitions, skating with three different partners during that time. In 1983 the USAC/RS inducted him into the Athletes Hall of Fame and in 1993 he was named to the Coaches Hall of Fame.

George Grudza was a record setting speed skater, with a great start, passing ability, and outstanding endurance. These assets allowed him to win the 1957 and 1958 Junior Men's title. Grudza advanced to the Senior division and won the Senior Men's title in 1960. Coming out of retirement in 1964, he again won the National Senior Men's Title. He set speed records that lasted for more than 10 years.

Verna Picton and George Moore, 1937

Another excellent Senior man in the 1960s, Edward Perales, won the National Title three years in a row from 1961 to 1963. Perales became the first man to win three consecutive years since Nationals started in 1937. He set many records during his career and was almost unbeatable in the one mile event. A member of the World Congress Team in 1962, he won this International meet in the 440, 880, and in the one mile races. In 1981 *Skate* magazine named him a sports all star.

Mary Merrell won her first U.S. Indoor title in 1959. She repeated this in 1960 and 1961. She became the first woman speedster to win three titles in a row in Senior Ladies speed. She took a brief respite from skating and then returned to win again in 1964, 1966, and 1967. No one has ever won five Senior Ladies titles; Merrell's six titles record may never be broken. She went on to compete and win as a Relay team member and later as a Masters division speed skater.

Charles Wahlig (left) in exhibition race, 1950's

Richard Gustafson, a competitor from 1956 to 1969, began as a speed skater in the Boys divisions and then as he grew older became a Senior Speed and Figure skating champion. Gustafson won Juvenile C Boys speed in 1956, Junior Boys speed in 1963,

Intermediate Men's speed and Senior Four Men's Relay both in 1964. He also won Junior Boys Freshman Figures in 1963, Intermediate Junior Figures in 1964, and Senior Men's Figures World Class from 1967 to 1969.

Another Speed champion who also excelled in artistic skating, Pat Bergin, won his first National title in 1958 and then captured every individual title possible from 1965 to 1972. Bergin held the record for the most individual speed titles won by a racer, nine National Championship titles. He also skated on seven National Championship Relay teams. People regarded Bergin as an accomplished freestyle skater and he often placed at Nationals in the Senior Men's Singles during the 1960s.

From 1968 to 1976 Tim Small won a record of nineteen U.S. Indoor Speed titles in both Division and Relays. In 1975 and 1976 he won every event he entered in Nationals, with a sweep of all the Senior National titles. Small set four record times in 1974, four new records in 1975, and six more records in 1976 including one in every distance. In 1975 judges presented him with the finish line flag from the meet, an unprecedented tribute for his outstanding performance. He skated on the USA Speed Team in 1975 and 1981. He often skated relays with his brother Tom Small in the 1970s.

Tim Small, 1975

After Tim Small retired in the late 1970s Tom Peterson emerged as the heir to the speed throne in the U.S. The victories of speed skater Peterson not only gained his country medals and prestige at the International level of the sport, but they also effectively elevated roller speed skating into the consciousness of America. His inspiring four Gold Medal performance in roller skating's debut at the 1979 Pan American Games, for example, earned him national television recognition and interviews in such publications as *Sports Illustrated*. His new found fame helped a blossoming USA speed program grow. During the last half of the 1970s, USAC/RS undertook a massive restructuring of the USA speed program. Peterson, already a top competitor on the indoor circuit, became the most noteworthy product of this program which launched the USA Speed Team to the top of the world standings.

Peterson had no peers at the International level. A master at track racing, he claimed 19 medals in the World and Pan American competitions from 1979 through 1984, despite having to "sit out" in 1982 due to injury. Of these top International placements, Peterson won an incredible seventeen Gold Medal wins. In 1980, Peterson became the first American man to win a World Championship Individual Gold Medal (he won three) and the first to win the World Championship overall title.

Peterson became a top talent on the indoor scene. Representing the Tacoma Speed Club of Tacoma, Washington, Peterson gained over 20 National placements in the Senior Division from 1977 to 1983. Since his retirement in 1984, Peterson has operated a skate wheel manufacturing business (Hyper Wheels) in Huntington Beach, California.

Tom Peterson leading the pack, 1980

The latest artistic and speed champion, Jennifer Rodriguez, is the first female roller skater to qualify to the World Team in both art and speed events. She placed in Nationals in both World Class Figures and Speed. She placed second in the World in Figures and Speed in 1992, and in the World Road Championship in Rome. Jennifer placed second overall in the 1993 World Championship in Colorado Springs, behind another fine American female speedster, Heather Laufer.

In the 1980s the Muse brothers became the dynamic duo of speed skating. Dante and Tony Muse have dominated the Senior Men's events over the past few years, at both the National and International levels. The Muse brothers hail from Des Moines, Iowa, where their family owns and operates several rinks. At the 1993 World Speed Championships, Tony Muse won the 300 Meter Timed Trials and 500 Meters, placed second in the Men's 1500 meter, and second for the Overall. Dante Muse won the 3000 meters and the 10,000 meters, and teamed up with Tony Muse and Derek Parra of Dover, Delaware, another great men's speed skater to win first in the Men's 5,000 Meter Relay. Parra ended up as the overall World Champion, the title that Tony Muse held in 1992. In the 1995 Pan-Am Games, Parra brought home the Gold Medal for roller speed skating. Two speed skaters presently still maturing in the late 1990s toward future stardom are Chad Hedrick and Cheryl Ezzell.

Jennifer Rodriguez, 1993

In the 1990s, outdoor racing and in-line roller skates became very popular. Speed times on in-line skates have beaten most of the traditional quad skate times. Separate events have been established for in-line skaters, and in the 1990's the International Federation accepted in-line skating at World competition. Since more speed is the goal in racing, many of the top skaters switched to in-line skates. Although the idea of in-line skates has been around for over 150 years, the new designs of the 1990s equipment, including wheels, frame, and boot innovations, have greatly improved their speed efficiency. Dante and Tony Muse helped to make the transition from quad skates to in-line skates. Quad skate World Champions in the 1980s, they became the first World Champions on in-line speed skates in the 1990s. In the mid 1990s, Chad Hedrick now dominates speed skating in World Competition.

Dante (middle) and Tony (right) Muse

Chad Hedrick, 1996

10 ROLLER HOCKEY

Professional Polo Match as played on Foot Cycles. The W.S. Cleveland Model.

Since the beginning of sports history, men played games using sticks and balls. The Persians, 2000 B.C., played an early form of ground hockey and the Greeks, 500 B.C. were the first to be pictured in a hockey game with a curved stick and little ball like the modern game. The Sioux Indians played with a soft ball of moose hair covered with buckskin, and the natives of Chile played with a stone or wooden ball.

The name hockey may come from one of two sources: a French word "hoquet" meaning a curved shepherd's stick, or the Anglo-Saxon "hackie" meaning hacking at each other's shins. The English played a similar game on a field, called "bandy ball." The game became so popular among King Edward III's soldiers, who played bandy ball instead of performing their duties, that he banned the game in 1365. The King, fearing for the safety of his kingdom, publicly destroyed all the balls and sticks.

What about hockey on skates? Men played an unorganized game with no formed rules called "shinty" on ice as well as on a field in England, Scotland, Canada, and America.

In 1876, the game of polo (on horseback) was introduced to America via England and India. It was first practiced in New York and then in Newport, Rhode Island, both cities were early roller skating centers. The skaters copied the polo game at the rink. The first official roller polo game occurred in 1878 at the Denmark Rink in London, England.

Roller Hockey Team, 1870's

In 1882, a National Roller Polo League formed in Dayton, Ohio with teams in seven cities, and by 1884 the Massachusetts Roller Polo League began operating with 14 teams from the cities of Chelsea, Boston, Lowell, Salem, Glocester, Colburn, Brockton, Haverhill, Cambridge, Lawrence, and Lynn, Massachusetts. The league wrote rules, employed officials, made-up schedules, invented a patented goal cage, and came up with 700 dollars worth of medals and prizes for awards.

In 1886 many considered roller polo one of the "best governed and most scientific games in the world of sports." A National League of Roller Polo was established and rules of the play by Professor Fields adopted. The National League of Polo Players, one of the strongest sports organizations in America at this time, had over 100 members.

1878 Roller Hockey Illustration

Five players made up the team: a center, halfback, quarterback, and two rushers. The star of a team was called the rusher, the main offensive player and sports hero, akin to the quarterback in modern football. Fans penned stories, poems, and songs. Polo rushers gained notoriety for picking up and dating ladies at the rinks.

Top row middle: Harrison Fry, 1930s

Two four-woman roller hockey teams, 1930s

Harrison Fry of Richmond, Indiana became a professional roller polo player in 1907. He played for a team in San Francisco just after the earthquake in 1906 as a rusher. Fry liked to rush, but he also played defense. He described himself as a good sized fellow for such a rough sport, one had to be big.

In 1917 Fry was a member of the ASM Seeders in the Indiana League. The Seeders hailed from Richmond, Indiana and entered in a great rivalry with the Muncie team, often drawing 1,000 spectators to a game. Fry interviewed in 1974 when he was 85 years old, recalled the tempo of the game as very fast with a few interruptions for fouls. Roller polo was rougher than football. The referees allowed contact, but you could not hold an opponent or touch the ball. The ball was similar to a baseball with a wound cord center and a quarter inch hard rubber cover.

Fry used Henley's 1910 model skates, manufactured in Richmond, Indiana. The manufacturer cut off the clamps and bolted the skates to the sole of work shoes, and added pieces of car tire rubber around the toes to stop the ball from catching up under the wheels.

Roller hockey competition declined somewhat after this initial burst of interest with most players found on city streets and vacant paved areas. During the 1920's and 1930's, the New York City Recreation Department sponsored outdoor speed and roller hockey. Street hockey remains popular in urban areas in America.

From 1920-1940, various roller hockey teams and leagues operated in the United States. Roller hockey became popular in Europe at this time. Women also became active in the sport, with women's teams in America and National teams from Europe forming. Since 1924, seven countries held Roller Hockey Championships. While Italy and England reigned as dominant teams at the time, many attempted to increase world roller hockey participation. In 1936 the Federation International de Patinage a Roulettes (FIPR) held a World Hockey and Speed Championships. Although many countries were invited, only European countries were represented. The British Rink Hockey team won the 1936 World Title, and their ninth consecutive European title (1925-1936). Italy placed second, and Portugal third. The U.S., though invited to play, wanted to use ice hockey sticks and a puck rather than official curved sticks and a ball used in the World matches. The Europeans said "no puck" and the U.S. team did not participate. Puck hockey played on roller skates remained a popular game in the USA throughout the 1940s in the upper northern tier and in Canada. The popularity of the puck game endured in areas where ice hockey teams play and are promoted on television.

In 1939 the 14th European Hockey Championship was held in Montreaux, Switzerland. Advertised as the 2nd World Championship, only the usual seven European countries participated. England and Italy, the favorites once again met in the first round. After a close match, England won 4-1. At the end of the tournament England won first place with Italy second, Portugal third, France fourth, and Switzerland last.

Shortly after the formation of RSROA, the organization published a draft of official roller hockey rules in 1940. However due to World War II, it was not until after 1950 that roller hockey (ball and puck) competition became serious in the USA. In 1959, the RSROA authorized the American Roller Hockey Association with Joe Spillman of San Antonio, Texas named the first Commissioner. The year 1961 marked the debut of roller hockey at the National Championships.

1931 Mid-west league roller hockey champions

In 1961 roller hockey competition got off to a thrilling start. The Rolling Ghosts of Lubbock, Texas, defeated the Capital Comets of Austin, Texas. The game was held during the opening night of Nationals in Fort Worth, Texas. Elimination events were held during the day. In the finals the Rolling Ghosts won 4-3 in overtime. Other teams in the tournament included the Franklin Challengers (California), the VFW Rebels (Tampa, Florida), and the Longview Rol-0-Way Hockey Club (Longview, Washington).

Henry Black, J.G. Black, Johnny "Preacher" Black, Dickie Sisson, Bill Sisson, Edwin Sisson, and Lyndol Hall made up the team for the Rolling Ghosts.

From 1961-1966 the roller hockey sport grew. After five years of National competition, there were 111 hockey clubs formed, 568 registered as players, and 93 men became commissioned officials in the American Hockey Program. During the 1960s the RSROA negotiated with and returned to FIRS after a twenty-five year absence. The U.S. finally ready to field a competitive World Team, selected an eight man all-star squad to go to the 1966 World Hockey Tournament (FIRS) in Sao Paulo, Brazil, May 10-20, 1966.

The Rolling Ghosts

The squad was selected from the three top teams: Rolling Angels (formerly Rolling Ghosts), the Knighthawks from Port Neches, TX, and the Silver Wheels from Midland, TX.

Bill Sisson was informed that his team, the Rolling Angels, would form the nucleus of the USA team. Practice sessions began in February at the Cotton Bowl Rink in Dallas. After many days of work outs came the final team selection: Bill Sisson (player/coach), Dickie Sisson, Edwin Sisson, Lyndol Hall, Johnny "Preacher" Black, Dickie Thibodeaux, and Roy Huckaby. Ted Bielicki of Detroit, Michigan was named head coach and Bill Sisson team captain. The average age of the team was 27 years old and the average height and weight was 5'10" and 168 pounds.

Team USA trained three days a week (Wednesday, Friday, and Sunday) and 2 1/2 hours each day to try to mold a competitive team. The International rules differ from the American rules. Most of the differences concerned the goalie, David Sisson. The goalie, according to international rules could not wear a chest protector, had to serve his own penalty time, and he could face a penalty shot. Sisson was used to crouching down in the net and stopping hard shots on his chest, however, now he would have to stand up and pick off or block shots with his gloved hand, stick, elbows, or legs.

1966 World Roller Hockey Tournament

In May, the team made the 4,000 mile trip to the Ginasio Ibirapuera (Sporting Hall) in Brazil. More than 24,000 people attended a day. In addition to facing teams with more international experience, the U.S. players had troubles stopping and cutting because their wheels slipped on the cement surface. As a result the U.S. lost the first five games but made a come back to beat England 6 to 5. They lost one more game to Argentina 2-0 and then beat Switzerland. Only the games against Spain 8-0 and Portugal 13-2 were real routs against the Americans. Most of the other games remained competitive thanks to good playing and David Sisson's goal-tending. The United States gained the respect of the International hockey community and furthered the development of roller hockey in America. Spain finished first, Portugal second, and Argentina third in the tournament.

In 1984, Johnny "Preacher" Black was elected to the USAC/RS Athlete's Hall of Fame. He helped to organize a roller hockey league in Texas in 1949. A founding member of the Rolling Ghosts team, Black helped them win six consecutive titles (1961-1966). As a member of the USA World Team in 1966, he provided the experience, stability, and leadership needed for international competition.

In 1985, Dickey Thibodeaux was elected to the USAC/RS Athlete's Hall of Fame. As a member of the Port Neches Knighthawks, he scored the winning goal to defeat the Lubbock Rolling Ghosts. He played as a member of the

National Championship teams in 1966, 1967, 1968, 1970, and 1972. He served as co-captain of the USA Team in 1970.

The USAC/RS Hockey Association has fielded a World Hockey Team since 1966. The hockey program in the U.S. has grown each year. The Junior Olympic program includes hockey, designed to promote the sport in the USA to young skaters.

The American game of roller hockey has two separate divisions, ball and puck. The National Hockey League (NHL) has helped to increase interest in and popularity of ice hockey in North America in the puck division. Today both hardball and puck hockey are official divisions of American and World Hockey. Both games are played at the FIRS World Championships. Team USA are all-star teams made up of the National Championship winners plus other all-star players. And in 1999, the Pan Am games will host an in-line roller skate championship.

1990 USA World Roller Hockey Team

The 1996 USA World In-Line Hockey Team

11   STAGE AND SHOW SKATING

World-Famous Two Kays, 1935

Stage and show roller skating dates back to the 1860s. William Fuller, an ice and roller skater, toured the world giving exhibitions on roller skates from 1865 to 1868. He amused and entertained general audiences, native Princes, nobility, and even the Czar of Russia. At the same time Jackson Haines was also exhibited on skates all over Europe.

Stage performing on roller skates proved popular from 1885 to 1930 in vaudeville acts, on stage, in a circus, or exhibitions of fancy skating in rinks. William (Billy) Carpenter skated in exhibitions and managed rinks from 1907 to 1915 around Boston. Carpenter started as an ice skater but switched to roller skates at age 12. Employed early in his life as a skate boy, he learned "fancy and scientific skating" by professor H. T. Frennette, a great Canadian skater at that time. In 1907 Carpenter toured rinks in the eastern states, with bookings all over for the next season. He teamed up with Jack Carpenter and formed an act called, "The Yankee Clowns." They performed comedy and acrobatic skating and played the vaudeville circuit until 1911. Carpenter managed the Elm Rink in New Bedford, Massachusetts in 1911 and began touring again in 1912. He worked for Fred Muree at the Select Rink in Augusta, Maine, and managed other rinks in that area until 1915. He also signed for a 20 week tour with the Helen Carlos Trio on the vaudeville circuit.

William (Billy) Carpenter

The duo of Howard Fielding and Helen Carlos performed in shows from 1915 through the 1920s. The Western Skating Association in 1915 recognized Carlos as "the greatest woman skater in America." Fielding and Carlos toured the U.S., Canada, and Europe. Their act dates back to 1908 and many considered it one of the best roller skating acts to play rinks or vaudeville in America. Fielding began as a solo act in 1902 doing fancy, trick, and speed skating. Very few skaters could defeat him in a half mile race. When Carlos joined the act in 1908, it became a roller dance and graceful skating routine. Her costumes were considered beautiful and the routines very original. Their home was Milwaukee, Wisconsin, but they toured America and Europe.

The Rexos, Edward Smith and later his wife, a well known roller skating act from 1884 to 1920, performed fancy, trick, and pairs skating on stage, in rinks, and at other public events all over the world. Edward Smith put on his first pair of skates in 1881. He worked as a skate boy at the North Division Street Rink in Michigan. He began doing local exhibitions in 1884 and in 1886 performed on the vaudeville circuit with the Rexford Troupe where he got the Rexo name he used for the rest of his career. He added his wife to the act in 1898 and they performed for 30 weeks with a traveling circus. The Rexos then performed their roller skating act in vaudeville, parks, fairs, and rinks from 1899-1903.

On December 7, 1903 they appeared as the opening attraction at the

The Rexos

new Coliseum Rink in Chicago before 5,000 people. This was at the start of another skating boom period in America. The Rexos opened rinks, played fairs and carnivals until 1908. The pair performed in rinks and theaters throughout England and Germany, where they played at the London Hippodrome and the Apollo Theatre in Nuremburg. The Rexos returned to the U.S. in 1910 and continued to tour on the vaudeville circuit for many years.

The Skating Franks, Charles L. Frank and his daughter Lillian, reigned as one of the greatest skating teams in the world from 1901 to 1921. Charles also skated with Nellie Donegan on the vaudeville stage. The Skating Franks opened a skating rink in California on the very night of the San Francisco earthquake in 1906. They traveled abroad in 1908 and skated in Cuba, South America, Europe, and Russia, returning to the United States at the out break of WWI in 1914. The pair skated on the vaudeville circuit until 1921. Charles Frank started his roller skating career in the 1880s and became well known in America and Europe as one of the best skating acts on tour.

Miss Adelaide D'vorak started skating as a school girl in 1906 placing first in the City Championship Race of Cleveland, Ohio, out of 18 contestants. She then engaged in a series of match races with local girls, and went undefeated. She beat Anna Miller, the Ohio State Speed Champion that same year, and next defeated the female champion of West Virginia. D'vorak won against her so soundly she then challenged all of the men skaters in the rink to race, defeating each one! She received an invitation to go to Mobile, Alabama to race. Her success there in defeating all comers made her fame spread through out the South, and gained a reputation as one of the greatest women speed skaters in America at that time.

Adelaide D'vorak

In 1909, D'vorak took up fancy and trick skating and soon became recognized as a bona fide attraction. Another success occurred in 1910 at the Madison Square Garden in New York City where she defeated every male skater that was matched against her in racing.

In 1910, D'vorak accepted a contract with the American Rink Company to go to Europe. She spent three years skating throughout the principal cities in England, Russia, and North Africa. She raced and performed exhibitions, but the strain began to affect her health. She returned to America, devoting her skating to fancy exhibitions and dancing on skates on the vaudeville circuit. She is remembered as one of the most artistic roller skating acts in the world.

Earl and Inez Van Horn teamed up to be one of the biggest roller skating attractions in the world. They started skating together in 1918. Earl was already an established roller skating entertainer. As a team they toured the world performing before royalty and heads of state. In America they became vaudeville favorites, and packed houses everywhere. They opened the Mineola Rink in New York in 1934 and developed some outstanding dance and figure skating clubs.

Jack and Caroline Dalton were also a well known vaudeville roller skating act during this period. Later they were partners in the Cleveland, Ohio Rollercade Rink, that was home to many fine skaters and was the site of several RSROA National Championships.

The National Museum of Roller Skating has memorabilia, costumes, and skates from all of these acts. Vaudeville and fancy skating exhibitions from 1870 to 1940 were one of the ways that roller skating was promoted at that time.

Earl & Inez Van Horn performing on a platform in New York, 1928

In 1942 a professional roller skating show formed in Chicago. Edward Smith, a well known skating supporter and later skating book publisher, promoted a beautiful young skater, Gloria Nord. He took Nord around to local rinks to present awards and to do promotional activities for skating in 1940-1941. Formally trained in ballet, she wrote articles in *Skating Review* magazine (1942-43) on ballet for skaters.

The Skating Vanities began its rehearsals at the Arcadia Rink in Chicago. A small show at first, it opened at the Coliseum in Baltimore, Maryland, on January 7, 1942. Admission was $1.65. The original name of the show, the Roller Follies, soon changed to the Skating Vanities and stayed with the name for the next decade. Gloria Nord was the first star of the Vanities and Harold Steinman from New York owned of the show.

Betty Lytle, one of the best roller skaters of her time, joined the show for a short duration, when it opened at Cleveland Arena on January 18, 1942. The show sold out. The production costs were $100,000, with $25,000 invested just in the costumes and a cast of 85 skaters. As the show continued to tour the skating numbers matured greatly. The Skating Vanities became a truly professional show in every aspect.

Gloria Nord

As the show toured and became well known around the country, many champion roller skaters joined to become stars. Ann Manion, Melva Block Moreno, Dolly Durkin, Ted Shufflebarger, Doug Breniser, Nancy Lee Parker, Caroline and Tony Mirelli, Peggy Wallace, Norman Latin, and Ronnie Brown—a Canadian Champion, were among those who performed with the Skating Vanities. Auditions were held around the country for other roller skaters to try out for the chorus numbers.

The Skating Vanities traveled all over the United States and made five European tours. At first, the show just included skating, but in the 1950s other non-skating acts were included to add variety to the performances. Even the great trumpet player, Louis Armstrong, at one time performed with the Vanities.

In 1955, the Vanities went on another trip to Europe. While in Germany, producer Harold Steinman saw and purchased a dancing waters machine. Fountains, streams of water, colored lights, and music were the feature of this entertainment, and display then added to the show. Later, Tony Mirelli used a dancing waters machine of his own design in the Roller Skating Spectacular at the National Championships.

During the 1955-1956 season, the Skating Vanities went to South America. Many of the American skaters, including the Mirelli's, retired from the show at this time. The Skating Vanities closed following the 1956 season.

The Roller Skating Spectacular started in the 1960s, a show produced in conjunction with the RSROA/USFARS Nationals. Tony and Caroline Mirelli directed and played instrumental roles in organizing and producing these wonderful skating shows. The Mirelli's included champion skaters of the previous year as stars. Various clubs around the country produced a variety of production numbers for the show held on the first evening of the USFARS National Championships. The Mirelli's, whose expertise in show skating was widely acclaimed, used show props, as well as Tony's dancing waters, to provide a great evening of skating entertainment.

Dolly Durkin

Budd Van Roekel, Red Shattuck, and Joe Nazzaro promoted the first Gold Skate Classic, held in Bakersfield, California in 1965. A show competition, various clubs and individuals presented show numbers with prizes awarded to the best singles, dance couples, pairs, and group production routines. The Gold Skate Classic is still held every year, and many club skaters and champion skaters started their career in this annual event. 1995 marked the thirtieth anniversary of the Gold Skate Classic.

Many amateur skating clubs in the USA hold annual skating shows, a good way to feature show skating and entertainment over difficulty and content in the performance. Everyone in the club can participate and enjoy the experience of performing on skates. Club shows have been in existence since the 1930s as a way to promote roller skating to the public.

Caroline and Tony Mirelli

Gold Skate Classic Program

12 SKATING SCHOOLS

Dick McLauchlen

The first skaters had to learn how to roller skate. Many of the ice skaters simply switched their skills to wheeled skates. Robert John Tyers opened and operated the first roller skating school in 1823 on a tennis court on Windmill Street in North Central London to teach people how to use his new skate, the Volito.

The next year in Bordeaux, France, after the success of the play which showcased skating scenes "La Laitiere Suisse," Robillon founded a skating school outdoors on paved surfaces to teach roller skating during good weather.

Jean Garcin, in 1828, constructed a gymnasium in Paris called The Cingar School, to teach people how to use the Cingar skates he invented. He taught group lessons and skating sessions. Then in 1849, Monsieur Constant built a gymnasium open to the public for roller skating lessons. Skates at the time, however, due to their poor quality, resulted in many accident and injured patrons. Though popular places, both roller skating establishments soon closed.

Soon after 1863 when James Plimpton introduced the "rocking skate," he opened skating schools, with lessons available at the rinks operated by the Plimpton Company. Plimpton had a proficiency test program where skaters could pass skating tests or learn from teaching professionals. Most other rinks in the 1880s and 1890s had professors to teach lessons and manage the rink in speed, hockey, and artistic skating, then called "fancy and scientific," skating programs.

The Plimpton Proficiency Skating Medal, 1866

When Perry Rawson introduced the International Style to America in 1938, there were very few skating teachers. Most knowledgeable teachers had learned from ice skating and were self taught by reading books by T. D. Richardson on the sixteen positions of figure skating or the book by Willie Boeckl, *On Figure Skating*. There were also some "flip books" available showing World Champion Karl Schaefer executing his figures and loops. One could flip quickly through the photos of the book and get a crude animation of the movements to do the school figures.

After Rawson brought the Lidstones to America on tour, he built a small rink on his estate in Asbury Park, New Jersey. He called it his skating laboratory, and invited interested teachers and skaters there to discuss the technique and theory of roller skating. As a result of Rawson's laboratory, several successful teachers developed large group lesson programs including Fred Freeman, Louis Bargman, and Fred Martin in the 1940s. Roller skating began to develop and the first Gold Medal tests were held in 1946. Though ice skating judges often rated roller skating performances in the early years, the RSROA soon sponsored commission programs to train judges in knowledge regarding roller skating.

Starting in 1943, Fred Bergin of Medford, Massachusetts, chairman of the RSROA Judges test and competition committee, held a skating school for teachers in four cities around the United States. Over 100 skating teachers took part in these RSROA professional schools with excellent information presented and discussions on skating techniques. The levels of skating and good teaching developed rapidly in the 1940s due to Fred Bergin's skating schools.

In the 1950s, other skating schools formed to help the teachers improve their skills at coaching. One of the first was held in Denver, Colorado, and later in Wolcott, Indiana. These were held for several years to help teachers improve their knowledge about roller skating. J. W. Norcross, Dick McLauchlen, Tommy Lane, and Bob Irwin helped to lead the discussions.

Skating school at Arcadia Skating Rink, Detroit, Mich., 1947-48

USA Roller Skating currently holds annual judges conferences to teach commissioned judges new concepts and better insight into judging roller skating. These have been held at the Olympic Training center in Colorado Springs and in Las Vegas. Many judges from around the country attend these seminars. USA Roller Skating also started a coaches certification program to help roller skating coaches keep up with the latest rule changes and new information on sports science and roller skating technique.

The oldest continuous roller skating training center in America is the Stroudsburg Roller Skating Camp at the Big Wheel Rink in Pennsylvania. Thousands of skaters have attended the training sessions, seminars, and judge's classes held there. Lou Ann Rinker began the camp in 1980, and it has operated every summer for the past 17 years. Many fine coaches have attended to give their knowledge on roller skating, including Ron Jellse, Charles Kirshner, Betty Hinkel, Donald Myers, John Daney, James Turner, Angie Famiano, David Golub, Bill Kilby, Al Taglang, Ann Wahlig, and Elvin Griffin.

Another well known skating center exists in Garmisch, Germany. It has operated for many years with skaters from Europe, America, and South Africa training there in the International Style skating. Other training centers held in recent years include ones in New Bedford, Massachusetts, the Great Lakes Training Center in Palatine, Illinois, the New England Center in Connecticut, and the Virginia Beach Training Center.

Jack & Irene Boyer - 1942 American Senior Dance Champions

USA Roller Skating has held an International Artistic Skating Academy at the Olympic Training Center in Colorado Springs since 1988. Many top skaters with ability and potential attend this week long training camp to study with coaches from the USA and Europe. There are seminars and practice times in dance, figure, freestyle, and pairs skating as well as supplementary sessions in choreography, sports medicine, and sports science. The skaters live and train at the U.S. Olympic Training Center facility with athletes from the other Olympic sports. New skating champions benefit greatly from the use of this facility and the USA Roller Skating programs held there for artistic, speed, and hockey.

Stroudsburg Roller Skating Camp, 1996

13 ROLLER SKATING MUSIC

Sheet Music for "Rollin' On Our Roller Skates," Copyright 1933

As near as historians can determine, roller skating originated in Europe in the early 1700s, likely as an experiment intended to extend the ice skating season or to move ice skating indoors during a period prior to the creation of artificial ice. This movement occurred more than 100 years before the creation of commercial roller rinks. Early roller skating incentives entertained and amused fashionable European salons, as well as to portrayed skating in the theater. Many have heard the classic story, related in this book, of the mechanical inventor Joseph Merlin roller skating at a posh party in London in the 1760s while playing the violin and crashed into a large mirror, causing extensive damage to it and him. From the beginning, music played an important but sometimes distracting roller skating function.

The music that played in early roller rinks largely consisted of live performances by brass bands. Professional instructors were hired, exhibitions presented and dance movements performed on roller skates, including "The Promenade Step," "On To Richmond," "The Philadelphia Twist" and more. *Spalding's Manual of Roller Skating*, 1884, stated "Expert skaters will find no trouble in learning to waltz or go through the movements of quadrilles on rollers. A thorough proficiency in the movements will enable the skater to acquire with comparative ease the necessary steps for waltzing."

Brass bands continued to flourish within the more affluent rink facilities in larger cities into the next century. This popularity of brass bands spread throughout the United States and into Europe. The music and the skating became a popular attraction even to non-participants. Quoting from a contemporary author, Morris Traub, in his 1944 edition of *Roller Skating Through The Years*, skating "naturally draws to itself an attendance composed of the best people in the city, and great care is taken by the management that nothing shall occur to mar the sense of refinement or propriety entertained by an audience of this character. The Casino Rink in Chicago will seat 3,000 spectators on the main floor and in the gallery and private boxes." The music is furnished by the band of the First Regiment I.N.G., directed by Professor Austin, a coronetist of no mean note, and whose excellent quality is his adaptability.

As roller skating entered the 1900s, it experienced fluctuations in popularity as more working class people acquired a measure of leisure time and high society tired of the pastime. Some of the social elite found it less than decorous to end up on their behinds in the middle of the rink floor, to the amusement of their contemporaries. Such accidents lead to sport defections. Rinks found it necessary to conserve resources as their customer base shifted to less affluent patrons and at times because of lessened participation. The expensive orchestras that formerly provided musical accompaniment for roller skating proved too expensive for the tightened budgets of the rinks. The newly invented mechanical band organ and early electric organs replaced the brass bands and orchestras, providing the oomp-pa-pas for roller skating rinks. The early band organs operated from compressed air and used music rolls much like player pianos, advertised as "superior in tone and volume to any rink band or any other make organ." Manufacturers of the organs supplied the latest popular tunes on roll music

Military Band—46 Keys
With Bass and Snare Drums and Cymbal
Style 46, Cylinder-Played Style 146, Paper-Played
8 Music Selections 18 Music Selections

Employee of C. M. Lowe's portable roller rink operation standing next to the Wurlitzer organ, 1920's.

and were very well received by the owners. As late as the 1950s, a rink in downtown Cleveland used a band organ situated in the center of the floor.

Roller skating required a solid musical beat so that dancing couples could synchronize their skating steps. The penalty for missteps was a crashing fall to the floor, so there was less tolerance for rhythm subtly on behalf of skate dancers of modest ability. Another early musical score was the Deagan "Electric UnaFon" used in rinks around the country. This instrument played from a keyboard and was advertised as "weather proof, fool proof, always in tune, unique and makes every patron a repeater." It was said that the instrument's "volume was enormous and tone entrancingly beautiful. The tone is in quality, rousing and exhilarating to such an extent that it puts life in the feet of skaters."

Contemporary entertainment in America of the 1920s, 30s, and 40s, organ music was played on every radio station, as background music for the soaps (then on radio) and general fill-in music. Quite popular in general, organ music also proved popular at roller skating rinks.

Many stations had their own organist to play musical interludes from time to time when a local station lost its feed from the network in New York or Chicago. Many homes at the time commonly had a piano and/or a organ. Sheet music sold as well or better than recorded discs and every department store had a sheet music section. Some of the larger, more affluent rinks with the space for the pipes and the patience to keep them all in tune installed theater pipe organs. The Wurlitzer Organ, the grand-daddy of them all, had the facility to entirely duplicate a brass band with one man at the keyboard. In the 1940s and 50s, numerous rinks owned Wurlitzer Organs or other pipes, such as the Oaks Rink in Portland, Oregon, the Elmhurst and Hub Rinks in Chicago, the Arena Gardens and Arcadia Rinks in Detroit, the Rollercade in Cleveland and many others.

Don Simmons, organist at the Oaks Amusement Park, Portland, Oregon, circa 1950's

The 1930s, 40s, and 50s remained the Hammond Electronic Organ. It could be played with a solid beat for roller skating, took up little space, required little more maintenance than a radio, and had the flexibility of tone and rhythm to adapt to all of the roller skating tempi in common use for roller skating dances. In the late 1930s, urged on by Wall Street millionaire, Perry Rawson, rinks adapted European ice dances to roller skates. The practice spread like wildfire throughout the United States. Every rink of importance employed teaching staff to show patrons new steps and to incorporate the performances of waltzes, tangos, fox-trots, two-steps, etc., as "dance specials" in the evening programs.

One must remember that the 1930s and 40s were the era of the big bands and ballroom dancing. This popular music easily transferred from the dance hall to the roller rink via Hammond and pipe organs, played in strict tempi to regulate precision of the couple and pace within the skating center.

Roller skating rinks proved extremely popular with adults as well as children, although children had less money to spend. The dances, both simple and complex, acted as a social mixer within the rink to create new friendships and establish a club-like atmosphere with regular patrons. Many rinks in the larger cities would not admit children to evening sessions, as it interfered with adult recreation.

Many rinks without sufficient funds, space or commitment to maintain a pipe organ, chose to add various keyboard instruments to their Hammond organ to increase its musicality. Electronic rhythm sections including such branded attachments as "Novacord" and "Solo-Vox" were attached to Hammonds in roller rinks, long before these organ enhancements became built in to modern transistor keyboards and electronic gadgetry. These rinks pointed with pride to their musical programs which featured the Hammond organ with Novacord. As organ music became less popular in the 1950s and 60s to the American public, with radio less programmed and more DJ (disc jockey) oriented, many people came to identify organ music with "rink music." That is, until the rinks slowly began to abandon organ music in favor of more contemporary recorded music.

Russell Bice at the console of the Wurlitzer Pipe Organ at the Arena Gardens

Not all rinks sold their Hammond organs, particularly those with well-established adult clientele. The old timers still wanted to hear organ music and skate dances, but the kids wanted rock and roll. A lot of rinks compromised between the two, setting aside two or three nights a week when they played organ music, attracting largely adult patrons. While diminishing slightly every year, this trend continued through the 1960s and early 70s, until the advent of disco roller skating.

Disco music, with a strongly emphasized beat, easily transferred to roller skating in a free-form manner, without defined dance steps. It encouraged "doing your own thing" movements and an unformatted "strolling" style of roller skating. Girls and boys, men and women, flocked to the rinks because disco roller skating was "IN." Hollywood stars roller disco danced. For many rinks, disco landed the final blow that pushed out organ music altogether. A rink no longer needed special non-contemporary dance skating programs; in fact, during the disco era, the bulk of customers refused to tolerate it. Rink managers found it easier and more popular to simply open the doors and let the disco music attract patrons. But when the disco craze ended in 1981, many of the skate dancers that performed to organ music no longer skated.

Marie Schram played the organ for the Sefferino Roller Rink, Cincinnati, Ohio, 1950's

Disco roller skating was not really a new phenomenon. The Capehart Orchestrope phonograph amplifier and speaker system was developed in the late 1920s. Capehart was only one of many such manufacturers of electronic sound equipment that advertised "unusual range and volume for music." When recorded music on 78 rpm shellac discs evolved from "acoustic" recording to electronic, the sound greatly improved from when the great tenor Caruso hollered songs into an inverted megaphone at the turn of the century. Electronic recordings lead to electronic reproduction and greatly magnified sound levels.

The power amp was invented and its application adapted to roller skating. Initially in the 1930s and 40s, organ music was amplified in most rinks, and some of it quite badly: the old shellac discs wore out with the static and surface noise greatly amplified. But this did not dampen the ardor of the skate dancers.

Hi-fi music was not introduced to roller skating until much after the advent of 45 and 33 rpm microgroove records. In the late 1960s owners and operators began developing high fidelity sound systems in their rinks, using the latest speakers and reproduction technology. Power amps grew larger and speakers strategically situated all over the rink for uniform musical clarity.

In the 1980s post-disco era, rink owners found that the loud, sometimes raucous, popular music of modern times drove away most of remaining adult skaters. Rock and roll music did not prove very adaptable to dancing on skates in the old-time sense. The traditionalists disappeared. Many believe that after adults left, teenagers abandoned roller skating too, as it became increasingly identified as "kid's stuff."

Not only is the music of the Billboard Top 100 less appealing to adults, the current unregulated nature of session skating where the younger majority is often engaged in unpredictable movement, makes the roller skating scene somewhat more risky for the uninitiated adult. They can not relate and stay away.

Roller Disco Fever

In the last 30 years, roller skating changed from traditional adult entertainment to one almost exclusively as children's recreation, in terms of public participation in session roller skating. For the previous 200 years, music was the mucilage that pasted together commercial recreational roller skating as an adult industry. The evolution of rink music may be responsible for the demise of adults from public skating sessions. Furthermore, the absence of formal and even informal rink dancing programs that serve to initiate social contact, may now discourage integration of newcomers to the rink's social fabric and activities. The absence of formalized programming offers no incentive for patrons to improve their skating ability and remain involved with the rink as their main recreational resource.

Dominic Cangelosi, Magician of the Keyboard and 1996 USA Roller Skating Distinguished Service Hall of Fame Inductee, has been providing dance music at the United States Championships for over twenty years.

14 ARTISTIC SKATING COSTUMES

De Sylvia & Irene, Artistry on Wheels, 1918

Over the years, skating costumes became increasingly functional. At first, skaters wore their regular clothes for general skating. The men's costume (1865-1885) were pants and a jacket. Women wore bustled, full length dresses which, though fashionable, proved very restrictive to their skating. Women never wore slacks for skating before 1920.

The average age of champion skaters around the turn of the century was higher than today, skaters averaging 16 to 18 years old today, while earlier champions were usually in their twenties or thirties. Their clothing reflects their age difference.

During the 1924 Winter Olympic Games in Chamonix, France, Sonja Henie of Norway, then only 11 years old, skated her first Olympics. She entered as the Norwegian Champion to gain experience for the future. A child skater never competed against mature adults before in International skating. Her dress was that of a child--above the knee! All of the other women skaters wore medium or full length skirts.

Although Henie did not win, one judge placed her first in the freestyle section of the competition. She had freedom and youthful athletic jumps and spins the others could not execute because of their long skirts. This event marked the introduction of the short skating skirt that all women skaters now wear.

In the 1930s, men wore dark ballet tights and a jacket. After World War II, pants were worn. Not until the 1960s, when new stretch fabrics became available, did men gain the freedom of leg movement without baggy pants.

Another fashion change for men came in 1964 when men's costumes changed from the highly decorated, sequined, jump suits to a more formal tuxedo type costume with very little trim allowed. Today men wear stretch jump-suits, open collar shirt or a tie for figure and free skating. The dance costumes are still more formal with a short coat and pants with a tie, pin or ascot. A few male dancers wear tuxedo tails on the jacket. Sequins in moderation are reappearing on a few male costumes at the International level.

Today women wear stretch fabrics in a leotard cut with a very short attached skirt to cover the tights. Figure costumes tend to be more conservative in decoration and cut, while freestyle and dance dresses are more often colorful and adorned with sequins, crystals, and auroras.

The non-competitive skaters or social skaters usually wear comfortable, in-style fashions. A beginner or outdoor skater should wear durable clothes that will not be easily ruined after a few falls. Cotton pants or jeans are usually acceptable. Warm-ups and jogging suits are comfortable and practical for practice in outdoor skating. Polyester and lycra are also popular fabrics but holes will melt in the fabric when friction with the skating surface occurs. Most skating centers have posted dress rules on good taste.

Postcard, 1907

Sonja Henie, 1932

1940s

During years America engaged in World War II, 1942-5, most adult men were in the service. This photograph shows Ladies Pairs. The girls wore matching outfits and performed free style, lifts, and shadow pairs skating in the USARSA. (Left to right) Nancy Reuter and Patricia McCormack (1st), Shirley and Charlotte Ludwig (2nd), and Doris Harrington and Marion Holzhauer (3rd).

Albert Shady and Dorothy Luginbuhl, from Mineola, NY won the 1943 USARSA Senior Mixed Pairs. Shady wore a short tuxedo jacket, cummerbund shirt, and a bow tie. Luginbuhl wore a velvet dress with sheer sleeves and a row of sequins at the neck line.

In the 1940s Figures and Freestyle events were combined; figures for elimination and freestyle for finals. In figure events men wore a white shirt and tie or a sweater. Bill Reed, 1st Place, (left) was wearing his freestyle costume - satin shirt, cummerbund, and ballet tights. Frank Salvage is in the middle (2nd Place) and Jack Dalton on the right place third.

1950s

James Mohler, the 1957 Senior Men's Freestyle champion, wore this jumper outfit with matching boot covers. On his chest, a star burst of sequins that continued down his left pant leg.

Dance outfits in the 1950s became more decorated. The men's jacket lapels were either trimmed or entirely sequined. The ladies skirts were full but shorter than the 1940s. Men wore short jackets that had a formal look with a shirt and bow tie. Men started wearing boot covers to match the pant material and color. Robert & Joan LaBriola, champions in American Senior Dance from 1950-1953.

The 1950s men's freestyle costumes become highly decorated with sequins. Often the design would reflect the musical selection of the skater such as the eagle on the chest of the skater on the right. The skater in the center is Jerry Bruland, 1949 Junior Boys Freestyle champion.

1960s

In the 1960s the Esquire Dance division (35 & up) was added to the RSROA competitive program. The ladies had to wear full skirts below the knee by regulation. The rule later changed and the Esquire Ladies were allowed to wear shorter skirts. The 1963 American Esquire Dance Champions were Bill Romain & Frances Romain who were interviewed by an ABC commentator.

(Left) The 1960s ladies figure costumes were very conservative, tailored with few decorations. Debra Niezer, 1969 Freshman Girls Figure champion, has only a few stones around the collar and cuffs.

(Right) In 1964, there was a move to more conservative costumes, especially for men. The requirement became a dark color or white, tuxedo cut outfit with a white shirt and tie or a turtleneck shirt; no sequins were allowed. Shown in the picture are: Cecilia Darimont Kelley and Gerry McNieve who is wearing a classic 1960s black dance outfit.

In the 1960s there were roller skating spectacular shows during the opening night of the championships. In this photograph, Richard St. Hilaire and his free dance partner, Nancy Lumpkin, perform under the spotlights. The lady's dress is all sequin fabric and St. Hilaire is wearing the dark tuxedo, shirt, and tie.

1970s

Three men's medalists at the 1972 World Meet: Lienhard Leonard (Switzerland), Michael Obrecht (Germany) and Randy Dayney (USA). They all wore dark tux outfits, shirt, tie, or turtle neck. The pants were tight fitting and made from stretch material. There were no decorations except for the patch on the sleeve.

In the 1970s, men began to wear jumpers, shirt, and tie for figure skating. Pictured is Ronald Milton, the RSROA Figure champion in 1971, skating in International Style Senior Men's Figures.

This group picture of the 1977 World Artistic Team gives a good idea of all the styles of the 1970s. The Freestyle, Pairs, and Dance Teams are shown. The Dance Teams have their Free Dance outfits on. They wore the tux outfits during the compulsory section of the competition.

1980s

Steve and Harriet Siegmann skated Free Dance in 1988. The trim design is the same for both outfits. However, Harriet's is done in sequins while Steve's is in shiny lame material. In the U.S. men could not wear sequins or stones.

1983 and 1984 World Class Dance Champions Angie Famiano and David Golub skated Free Dance. Angie's dress is made of all sequin material. David's top was shiny lame material for the U.S. meets. He also had a sequin top for World meets, where the rules were less strict regarding men's outfits and he could wear sequins.

In 1987 at the National Artistic Championships, Sarah Buck took home the bronze in Primary Girls' Singles. The Ladies Freestyle outfits have become highly decorated in the 1980s and 1990s. The basic leotard can not be French cut and the skirt is short but must cover the tights. Feathers, sequins, and stones are used extensively for decoration on the body of the outfit.

1990s

Eddie Byrd shown here at the 1996 U.S. Championships wearing a light-colored outfit with a high collar and lots of ruffles on the neck and cuffs. There are no stones or sequins. Men have gone away from the tuxedo outfit in the 1980s and 1990s. They wear a shirt and stretch skating pants for free style.

The Junior and Senior World Class team members wearing team uniforms at the 1996 World Championships in Mar del Plata, Argentina.

Brian Richardson and Amy York, competed in World Class Pairs at the 1996 U.S. Championships. Often a free dance or pairs outfit will reflect the style and mood of the music. Here skin-colored fabric gives the illusion of a two piece outfit on the lady. Notice there is some decoration reappearing on the men's costume.

BIBLIOGRAPHY

Boeckl, Wilhelm. ***Willy Boeckl On Figure Skating*** Moore Press, NY (1937).
Brooslin, Michael ed. ***American Roller Skates*** National Museum of Roller Skating, Lincoln, NE (1990).
Browne, G.H. ***Handbook of Figure Skating With 10,000 Figures to Practice*** Springfield, MA (1907).
Brown, Nigel. ***Ice Skating - A History*** Barnes, NY (1959).
Busby, T. ***Concert Room and Orchestra Anecdotes*** Vol. 2, London, England (n. d.).
Champion Skate Book and Complete Amateurs Guide NY Popular Pub. (1884).
Copley-Graves, Lynn. ***The Evolution of Dance on Ice*** Plantoro Press, Columbus, Ohio (1992).
Consumer Guide, ed. ***The Complete Book of Roller Skating*** Wallaby Book, New York (1979).
Dean, Fred and Joan, ed. ***Ice and Roller Skate Magazine*** 1 Strathmore Close, Caterham, Surrey, England. CR3 5EQ.
Dayney, Randy, with Joel H. Cohen. ***Winning Roller Skating*** Henry Regnery Company, Chicago, IL (1976).
Fetler, Camille, and Rolf Noess. ***History and Introduction to Roller Skating*** Published by FIRS. (1982).
Fitzgerald, Julian T. ***Skaters History On Ice and Roller Skating*** Western Skating Association, Chicago, IL (1916).
Goodfellow, Arthur. ***National Roller Skating Guide -1956*** National Sports Publications. NY (1956).
Harpers Monthly Magazine #239, The Story of William Fuller, 689-702. April, 1870.
Henley, M.C. ***Henley's Official Roller Polo Guide*** Richmond, IN (1885).
Historical Roller Skating Overview Published by the National Museum of Roller Skating, Lincoln, NE, 1982 to 1995.
Hollander, Z. and Clark, S. ***Roller Hockey: Sticks, Skates, and City Streets*** Hawthorne Books, NY (1976).
Illustrated London News Magazine London, England (1851).
Konner, Linda. ***Roller Fever*** Scholastic Book Services, New York (1979).
Lussoso, Gianni, ed. ***International Skating Magazine*** Via Marco Polo, 3. 65100 Pescara, Italy.
Matthews, Peter, ed. ***Guinness Book of World Records -1994*** Guinness Publishing Ltd. London & NY (1994).
Meagher, George A. ***A Guide to Artistic Skating*** T.C. Jack Ltd. London, England (1919).
Monahan, John J. ***Skater Magazine*** Endicott, NY (1975-1978).
National Museum of Roller Skating, 4730 South Street, Lincoln, NE 68506.
Nieswizski, Sam. ***RollerMania*** (history book in French, excellent graphics) Translated by James Turner, #128/ Decouvertes Gallimard, Paris, France.
Martin, Bob. ***Roller Skating*** A. S. Barnes and Company, New York (1944).
Mirelli, Caroline. Roller Vanities Scrapbook and Personal Memoirs (1995).
O'Neill, Edward R. ***Roller Skating*** Ronald Press Company, New York (1960).
Richardson, T.D. ***The Art Of Figure Skating*** A.S. Barnes, NY (1962).
Skate Magazine RSROA, National Museum of Roller Skating has a complete collection 1942-1989. Known as ***Skating Review*** in early issues.
Skating The official USFSA magazine, Colorado Springs, CO 1930-1995.
Smith, Beverly. ***Figure Skating A Celebration*** McClelland & Stewart Inc. Toronto, Canada (1994).
Smith, E. ***Instruction Book of Roller Skating*** Portland, Maine (1884).
Spalding's Official Roller Polo Guide, Including Fancy Skating American Sports Publishing Company. NY (1895).
Traub, Morris, ed. ***Roller Skating Through The Years*** W. Frederick Press, NY (1944).
Turner, James. ***History of Roller Skating*** RSROA, Lincoln, NE (1975).
United States Amateur Confederation of Roller Skating, Lincoln, NE.

> ***America Roller Dance Skating II***, Twelfth Edition, 1989.
> ***Dictionary of Roller Skating Terms*** 1980.
> ***Roller Figure Skating*** Eleventh Edition, 1989
> ***Roller Skating Coach*** 1992-1995.
> ***U.S. Roller Skating*** (official magazine) 1989-1995.

Wilhite, Scott, ed. & comp. ***Evolution of the Roller Skate: 1820 to Present*** National Museum of Roller Skating, Lincoln, NE (1994).

CREDITS

1 THE DEVELOPMENT OF SKATES, EARLY ORIGINS
p. 6 Sam Nieswizski, ***Rollermania***, Decouvertes Gallimard, 1991 (p. 10).
7 *Historical Roller Skating Overview (HRSO)*, Issue No. 15, September 1985, National Museum of Roller Skating (NMRS).
8 (top) Nieswizski, p. 14.
  (middle) Scott Wilhite, ***The Evolution of the Roller Skate: 1820 - Present***, 1994, p. 11, (NMRS).
  (bottom) Photograph courtesy of the Smithsonian.
9 (t) Wilhite, p. 13.
  (b) NMRS collection.
10 (t) Nieswizski, p. 18.
  (b) Nieswizski, p. 19.
11 (t) Photograph courtesy of the Smithsonian.
  (b) NMRS (10.76).

2 THE PIONEERS
12 Plimpton Collection (90.36), NMRS.
13 (t) Plimpton Collection (90.36), NMRS.
  (m) Wilhite, p. 23.
  (b) NMRS collection.
14 *Spalding's Manual of Roller Skating*, 1884.
15 Julian T. Fitzgerald, *Skaters History on Ice & Roller Skating*, 1916, p. 44.
16 Arthur Goodfellow, *Wonderful World of Skates*, pp. 7, 62.
17 NMRS collection.

3 THE EVOLUTION OF SKATES, 1863 TO PRESENT
18 Fitzgerald, p. 146.
19 (t) *HRSO*, Issue No. 10, June 1984, NMRS.
  (m) Wilhite, p. 66.
  (b) NMRS collection.
20 (t) Wilhite, p. 106
  (b) NMRS collection.
21-23 NMRS collection.

4 THE BOOM PERIOD, 1880-1910
24-26 Ludascher collection (90.42), NMRS.
27 *Spalding's Official Roller Polo Guide, Including Fancy Skating*, 1895.
28-30 James Turner drawings, 1995.
31 Armand Champa (80.6.50), NMRS.

5 SKATING ASSOCIATIONS
32 Western Skating Association, 1916.
33 (t) Fred A. Martin collection (82.54), NMRS.
  (b) C.W. Lowe (83.101.58), NMRS.
34 Richard McLauchlen (81.33.34), NMRS.
35 (t) *Skating Review*, December 1944.
  (b) NMRS collection.
36 (t) *Skating Review*, July 1942.
  (b) Chester Fried (94.7.26), NMRS.
37 NMRS collection.

6 ORIGINS OF SKATE DANCES
38 Elsbeth Muller (81.13.5), NMRS.
39-40 NMRS collection.
40 (b) Richard McLauchlen (81.33.116), NMRS.
41 Roller Skating News, January 1958, NMRS.
  (b) Betty Jennings (97.6.1), NMRS.
42-43 NMRS collection.

7 THE ORIGINS OF FIGURE & FREE SKATING
44 Richard McLauchlen (81.33.286), NMRS.
45 NMRS collection.
46 George Pickard (81.1.200), NMRS.
  (b) Richard McLauchlen (81.33.361), NMRS.
47 NMRS collection.
48 The World Figure Skating Museum, ***Skating Through The Years***, 1942.
  (b) Victor J. Brown collection (84.90.1), NMRS.
49 Richard McLauchlen (81.33.118), NMRS.
  (b) NMRS collection.
50 Sylvia Haffke (84.82.3), NMRS.
  (b) Richard McLauchlen (81.33.113), NMRS.
51 Rose L. Martin (82.46.122), NMRS.
  (b) NMRS collection.

8 PAIRS AND FOURS SKATING
52 Rose L. Martin (82.46.123), NMRS.
53 Richard & Marge McLauchlen (82.25.96), NMRS.
  (b) *Skating News*, June 1952.
54 NMRS collection
55 Rose L. Martin, (82.46.78), NMRS.
  (b) *Skating News*, June 1957.

9 SPEED
56 Richard McLauchlen (81.33.128), NMRS.
57 Al Kish (82.51), NMRS.
58 C.W. Lowe (83.101.108), NMRS.
59 Richard & Marge McLauchlen (82.25.43), NMRS.
  (b) Rose L. Martin (82.46.21), NMRS.
60 Rose L. Martin (88.22.6), NMRS.
  (b) M.M. Shattuck (82.97.4), NMRS.
61 C.W. Lowe (83.101.80), NMRS.
62 Richard & Marge McLauchlen (82.25.39), NMRS.

(b) Courtesy of Ron Miner.
63 Bill Henning (84.5.1), NMRS.
   (b) Rose L. Martin (88.22.3), NMRS.
64 Fred A. Martin collection (82.54), NMRS.
65 Bill Henning (84.47.8), NMRS.
66 Al Kish (82.95.1), NMRS.
   (b) NMRS collection.
67 Joe Wienmeier (96.59.70), NMRS.
   (m) NMRS collection.
   (b) Richard McLauchlen (81.33.336), NMRS.
68 Rose L. Martin (82.46.47), NMRS.
   (b) NMRS collection.
69 *Skate*, Fall 1975.
   (b) Ted Kirk, Roller Skating Rink Operators Association.
70 Proshots, USA Roller Skating.
   (b) USA Roller Skating.
71 USA Roller Skating
   (b) Proshots, USA Roller Skating.

10 Roller Hockey
72 Ludascher Collection (90.42.160), NMRS.
73 NMRS collection.
   (b) Ludascher Collection (90.42), NMRS.
74 Ernest St. Germain (83.15.10), NMRS.
   (b) C.W. Lowe (83.101.42), NMRS.
75 C.W. Lowe (83.101.13), NMRS.
   (b) Bill Sisson (82.125.4), NMRS.
76 NMRS collection.
   (b) Bill Sisson (82.125.8), NMRS.
77 NMRS collection.
   (b) USA Roller Skating.

11 Stage & Show Skating
78 Rose L. Martin (82.46.42), NMRS.
79 Bill Henning (84.8.9), NMRS.
   (b) Armand Champa (80.6.45), NMRS.
80 Armand Champa (80.6.52), NMRS.
81 Julie Kellman (96.71.4), NMRS.
   (b) Richard Young (82.2), NMRS.
82-83 NMRS collection.

12 Skating Schools
84 Richard & Marge McLauchlen (82.25.103), NMRS.
85 Elizabeth Plimpton collection (90.36), NMRS.
   (b) NMRS collection.
86 Rose L. Martin (82.46.112), NMRS.
   (b) NMRS collection.
87 Courtesy of James Turner.

13 Roller Skating Music
88 Ludascher collection (90.42), NMRS.

89 Al Flath collection, NMRS.
   (b) C.W. Lowe (83.101.119), NMRS.
90 NMRS collection.
91 Rose L. Martin (82.46.126), NMRS.
   (b) James D. Sterrett (82.72.8), NMRS.
92 Photograph courtesy of Trevor Brown.
93 USA Roller Skating.

14 Artistic Skating Costumes
94 Rose L. Martin (82.46.37), NMRS.
95 Photograph courtesy of The World Figure Skating Museum.
96 (t & m) Al Flath collection, NMRS.
   (b) NMRS collection.
97 NMRS collection.
98 (t, m-left, & b) NMRS collection.
   (m-right) Photograph courtesy of James Turner.
99 NMRS collection.
100 (t & b) Photographs courtesy of Ted Kirk
   (m) NMRS collection.
101 (t & b) Proshots, USA Roller Skating.
   (m) USA Roller Skating.

The Rolladium, Waterford, Michigan

Index

ABBREVIATIONS

AAU	Amateur Athletic Union	*USAC/RS*	United States Amateur Confederation of Roller Skating (formerly the RSROA)
ASU	American Skating Union		
FIPR	Federation International de Patinage a Roulette	*USA Roller Skating*	Formerly USAC/RS
FIRS	Federation Internationale de Roller Skating (formerly the FIPR)	*USARSA*	United States Amateur Roller Skating Association
ISU	International Skating Union of America	*USFARS*	United States Federation of Amateur Roller Skaters
NSA	National Skating Association of Great Britain	*USFSA*	United States Figure Skating Association
RSA	Roller Skating Association (formerly RSROA)	*USOC*	United States Olympic Committee
RSROA	Roller Skating Rink Operators Association	*USIC*	United States International Competition

Name Index

Able, Tim 54
Allegretti, Arthur 64-5
Allen, April 50-1
Allred, Margot 49
Anderson, Bob 55
Andrews, Eldora 53
Anselmi, Laurene 51
Armstrong, Louis 82

Bacon, Frank 59-60
Bargmann, Louis 36, 48, 85
Barney, Everett Hosmer 19
Bates, Justin 47
Baxter, Skippy 48-50
Bayles, Daryl 51
Bergin, Fred 40, 85-6
Bergin, Pat 69
Belazzi, Franz 15
Bell, Vivian 67-8
Benedict, Patricia 53
Best, Bill 53
Bick, Louis 67

Bielichi, Ted 76
Black, Henry 75
Black, J. G. 75-6
Black, Johnny "Preacher" 75-6
Blanchard, Allen T. 33
Block, Melva 48-9, 81
Boeckl, Willie 40, 47, 85
Boyd, Billy 99
Bradbury, Louis 59
Breniser, Doug 55, 81
Brice, Russell 91
Brinker, Hans 7
Brooks, Baba 42
Brown, Ronnie 81
Brown, Victor J. 34-6, 48, 60, 66
Bruland, Jerry 97
Bryant, Frank 62-3
Buck, Sarah
Bulleigh, Phyllis 53
Button, Dick 47, 50
Burton, Jack 42
Byrd, Eddie 101

Cangelosi, Dominic 93
Carey, Jesse 20, 59, 61, 63

Carlos, Helen 79
Carlson, Carl 63
Carpenter, Jack 79
Carpenter, William (Billy) 79
Carroll, Joseph 40
Carroll, Kevin 47
Carroll, Pat 55
Castro, Gary 42
Centaro, Mirian 41-2
Chappata, Ray 54
Chase, Kenneth 40
Christopher, Lloyd "Whitey" 60, 67
Chudy, Edward 67
Cioni, Roland 59-62
Clayton, Frank 57-8
Clark, Mary Lou 67
Clary, Robert 55
Clemens, Linda Mottice 42
Clinton, Skip 47
Cohen, Scott 51
Collier, Dennis 55
Colozzo, Warren 53
Constant, Monsieur 85
Coltrona, Leo 65
Craig, Donald 53

Craton, Curt 42
Crickmore, Mike 42
Cunniff, Helen 67
Cunniff, Mary 67
Czar Alexander II, 16

Dalton, Caroline 81
Dalton, Jack 81, 96
Daney, John 86
Darling, Jesse 31
Davidson, Harley 20, 58-9, 63, 65
Davidson, John X. 58-9
Davis, Cecil 53
Dayney, April 47
Dayney, Randy 99

Deemer, LaVeta 67
Dench, Robert 40
Dickens, Charles 14
Doing, Clayton 50
Donegan, Nellie 80
Donohugue, Joseph F. 58
Donovan, 58
Dorn, Maxine 55
Duerlein, Ada 53
Durkin, Dolly 81-2
D'vorak, Adelaide 80-1

Edwards, G. 59
Eglington, Arthur 59-62, 65
Ellsworth, Rick 51
Emanual, Arthur 67
Emanual, Bert 67
Ezzell, Cheryl 70

Fackler, Eli 22-3
Famiano, Angie 42, 86, 100
Farrell, Claire 42
Fielding, Howard 79
Findley, Steven 47
Fitzgerald, Julian T. 33
Fleece, Helen 67
Flick, Nancy 67
Fotch, Jack 59, 61
Fowlkes, Vernon 21
Frank, Charles L. 80
Frank, Lillian 80
Freeman, Fred 36, 85
Frey, Leopold 16
Fry, Harrison 74

Fuller, William 79

Gallagher, Barbara 41
Garcin, Jean 9, 45, 85
Giles, Perry 21
Godfrey, Leonard 67
Golub, David 42, 86, 100
Goode, F. P. 33
Graf, Bill 42
Graney, Pat Fogerty 42
Griffin, Elvin 86
Grudza, George 68
Gustafson, Richard 69
Gynese, Linda 42

Haffke, Henry 49
Haffke, Sylvia 49
Haines, Jackson 10, 15-17, 39, 47, 79

Hall, Lyndol 75-6
Haller, Carol 55
Haller, Kenneth 67
Hamel, Don 67
Hancock, Beatrice 67
Hancock, Virginia 67
Handyside, Vicky 55
Harless, Gene 50
Harmon, Leo 64
Harmon, Paddy 19
Harrington, Doris 96
Harris, Trudy 40
Harrity, Scott 51
Hawthorne, Claude 66
Hedrick, Chad 70-1
Henie, Sonja 95
Henley, Micajah C. 19
Henning, Bill 63
Hill, G. E. B. 40
Hill, Shirley 67
Hinkel, Betty 86
Hohenadel, John 22
Holzhauer, Marion 96
Hood, Tom 7
Horne, Richard 42-3
Houck, Gary 55
Huckaby, Roy 76
Hudson, R. H. "Duke" 36, 46

Irwin, Bob 86

Jacques, Michael 50-1
Jellse, Ron 55, 86
Jennings, Bettie 41
Jerue, Judy 55
Johnson, Armond 67
Jones, Robert 45

Kearns, Diane 54
Kelley, Cecilia Darimont 98
Ketter, Joe 67
Kilby, Bill 86
King Edward II, 73
Kimm, Leon 63
Kirshner, Charles 86
Kish, Al 60, 65-6
Klopp, Frank 64
Koch, Ruth Ann 55
Krechow, Paul 40
Kromis, Nancy 52, 55

Oaks Roller Rink, Portland, Oregon

LaBriola, Joan 42, 97
LaBriola, Robert 42, 55, 97
Lane, Tommy 86
Latin, Norman 50, 55, 81
Laufer, Heather 70
Law, Dorothy 54-5
Legrand, Louis 10
Leonard, Lienhard 99
Lewis, Lillian 67
Lidstone, Jimmy 20, 35, 40-1, 46, 48, 85
Lidstone, Joan 20, 35, 40-1, 46, 85
Little, Chuck 55
Lohner, 9
Lowe, C. M. 89
Ludington, Ron 50
Ludwig, Charolette 96
Ludwig, Fred 41
Ludwig, Shirley 96
Luginbuhl, Dorothy 96
Lumpkin, Nancy 98
Lutz, Alois 50
Lytle, Betty 44, 46, 81

Maddox, Eugene 58
Maher, Dudley 67
Manion, Ann 48, 67, 81
Mapes, Bruce 50
Marquardt, Caroline 67
Martin, Bill 53-4
Martin, Fred 20, 34-6, 59-63, 85
Matejec, John 21, 52, 55
McCormack, Patricia 96
McGinnis, Norman 67
McGowan, Everett 65
McGuire, Tim 51
McLauchlen, Richard 52, 84, 86
McMillan, Bill 53-4
McMillan, Margaret 46
McNeive, Gerry 98
Meade, Ellen 51
Mejia, Karen 54
Merlin, Joseph 7-8, 89
Merrell, Mary 68
Meyerbeer, Giacomo 9-10, 15
Miller, Anna 80
Miller, Walter 64
Milton, Ronald 99
Mirelli, Caroline 81-2
Mirelli, Tony 81-2
Moe, Ed 62

Mohler, James 97
Molla, Delores 22
Monier-Williams 45
Moore, Allie 58-60, 62
Moore, Louise 54-5
More, George 68
Muller, Elsbeth 38-9
Muller, George 39
Mullican, Rick 49
Munch, Joseph W. 59, 62
Muree, Fred "Bright Star" 56-8, 79
Muse, Dante 70
Muse, Tony 70
Myers, Donald 86

Nazzaro, Joe 21, 82
Neely, Thaddeus 20
Neizer, Debra 98
Nista, Jerry 50
Norcross, J. W. 86
Norcross, J. W., Jr. 50, 55
Nord, Gloria 49, 81

Obrecht, Michael 99
Olson, Marilee 55
Omelia, Jimmy 58
Ordson, William 65
Osmun, Walter 62

Pankey, Jane 42-3
Panno, Tom 55
Parra, Derek 70

Perales, Edward 68
Park, Chester 33-4
Parker, Nancy Lee 50, 81
Pate, William 55
Paulsen, Axel 47
Peters, G. 59
Peters, Rodney 59-60
Peterson, Tom 21, 69-70
Petitbled, Monsieur 8
Pfetzing, Anna Catherine 64
Pfetzing, Mrs. Henry 64
Picton, Verna 67-8
Pidgeon, 45
Plimpton, Henry Richardson 14, 20
Plimpton, James L. 12-14, 20, 33, 57, 85
Powell, P. F. 58-9
Pringle, James 55

Rawson, Perry 35-6, 40-1, 48, 85, 90
Ray, Joey 65
Recker, Frances 55
Reed, Bill 96
Reiff, Midge 66
Reuter, Nancy 96
Reznick, Erving 67
Rhodes, Hershel 67
Richard, Monsieur 39
Richardson, Brian 101
Richardson, Levant M. 18, 20
Richardson, T. D. 85
Ringwald, Bob 66
Rinker, Lou Ann 86

Chutes Skating Rink, California

Roberts, Marilyn 42
Robillon, 9, 85
Robovitsky, Gail 54
Robovitsky, Ron 54
Rodriguez, Jennifer 70
Romain, Bill 98
Romain, Frances 98
Rosdahl, Ted 46, 50
Ryan, Robert 46, 48

Saindon, Harold 67
Saladee, Cyrus W. 22
Salchow, Ulrich 47
Salvage, Frank 96
Schaefer, Karl 85

Sisson, David 75-6
Sisson, Dickie 75-6
Sisson, Edwin 75-6
Skinner, Kenneth 57
Small, Tim 69
Small, Tom 69
Smith, Alfred 25-31
Smith, Edward 79-81
Snowton, Fred 58
Snyder, Charles 19-20, 49
Snyder, Shirley 46, 49
Spillman, Joe 75
St. Hilaire, Richard 98
St. Jacques, Tony 47
Stakosa, Walter 22, 46

Uebel, John 67
Umbach, Connie 40

Van Horn, Earl 22, 36, 81
Van Horn, Inez 36, 40, 81
Van Lede, Maximillian Lodewijk 8
Van Roehel, Budd 82
Vandervell, H. E 45
Vassali, Vincent 67
Viardot-Garcia, Pauline 10

Wacker, Adolf 42
Wahlig, Ann 86
Wahlig, Charles 41-2, 68
Wallace, Peggy 81
Wally, Nathaniel 47
Walton, Charlie 58
Ware, Walter 19
Watson, Billy 35
Wermes, Frank 67
West, Joe 65
Williams, Margaret 53-4
Wilson, C. J. 58-9
Wilson, Charles 60
Winslow, Samual 19
Wintz, John L. 21
Witham, Maxwell 45

Redondo Roller Rink, Redondo, Washington

Schattenkirk, Clifford 41
Schierbaum, Harry 67
Schmidt, Katie 40
Schram, Marie 91
Schreiter, Karl 39
Schwartz, Virginia 67
Scott, Ernest 67
Scott, John Jr. 67
Seifert, Jack 49
Seltzer, Leo A. 66
Shady, Albert 96
Shattuck, Red 82
Sherman, "Midge" 59
Shufflebarger, Ted 49, 81
Sibenaler, Lawrence 59, 61
Sibley, Alder 54
Siegmann, Harriet 100
Siegmann, Steve 100
Simmons, Don 90
Sisson, Bill 75-6

Steinmen, Harold 82
Stenuf, Heddy 48-9
Story, J. B. 33
Stovall, Louis 55
Stricklen, Billy 55
Suwinski, Lynn 47

Taglang, Al 86
Taglioni, Paul 10
Tassinari, David 42, 54
Theiner, Edward 67
Thibodeaux, Dickie 76
Thorton, Austin 67
Toon, Richard 55
Towle, Bruce 50
Traub, Morris 89
Turner, James 86
Turner, Lesley 40
Tyers, Robert John 8, 85
Tyrell, Fred 59, 61

Yarger, J. A. 22
Yarrington, Betty Jane 40
York, Nancy 101

Subject Index
American Style, 36-7, 40-2
associations: Amateur Athletic Union (AAU), 36, 41; Amateur Hockey Association (Britain), 34; American Skating Union (ASU), 36-7; Federation Internationale de Patinage a Roulette (FIPR), 34, 66, 74; Federation Internationale de Roller Skating (FIRS), 47, 66, 77; International Skating Union of America, 33; Eastern Association, 33; New England Association, 33; Western Association, 33, 62-3; National Skating Association of Great Britain (NSA), 33-4, 39, 66; New York Roller Skating Association, 13, 33; Roller Skating

Rink Operators Association (RSROA), 22, 34-6, 40-3, 46, 60, 75-6, 81; United States Amateur Confederation of Roller Skating (USAC/RS), (formerly the RSROA), 23, 37, 62, 76-7, 86-7; United States Federation of Amateur Roller Skaters (USFARS), 36-7; United States Figure Skating Association (USFSA), 31, 33, 40; United States National Amateur Roller Skating Association, 36-7; USA Roller Skating (formerly the USAC/RS), 37; Western Skating Union, 33
Atlantic House Skating Resort, 13, 33

Ball bearings, 14, 20, 57-8; loose, 63-4; precision, 20, 64; Richardson Ball Bearing and Skate Company, 20
ballet, 8-10, 15-16, 53-4

Capenhart Orchestrope phonograph, 92
Chicago Roller Skate Company, 19, 21
children, 91-2, 95
combination skating, 29

Dances: 39-40
Deagan Electric Uniform, 90

Hammond Electric Organ, 90-1
Harley Davidson Skating Boots, 20
hockey, 37, 72-7: Amateur Hockey Association (Britain), 34; American Hockey Program, 76; American Roller Hockey Association, 75; "bandy ball," 73; British Rink Hockey, 74; hardball roller hockey, 74, 77; Longview Rol-O-Way Hockey Club, 75; National Hockey League, 77; rusher, 73-4; "shinty," 73
teams: ASM Seeders, 74; Franklin Challengers, 75; Rolling Angels, 76; Rolling Ghosts, 75-6; Team USA, 76; USA World Team, 77; VFW Rebels, 75
Ice skating, 7-8, 15-16, 23, 41, 45-6

International Style, 15, 36-7, 43

National Museum of Roller Skating, 15, 19, 49, 81

Olympic Committee, 34, 36-7
organs, 89-90: Hammond Electric, 90-1; Wurlitzer, 90

Pan Am Games, 37, 69-70
Plimpton Skate Company, 14
polo: horseback, 73; leagues, Massachusetts Roller Polo League, 73; National Roller Polo League, 73

Raybestos-Manhattan Company, 21
Raymond Skate Company, 58
"reverse rocking turn" motion, 45
Richardson Ball Bearing and Skate Company, 20
rinks: Arcadia Rink, 81; Arena Gardens, Detroit, 35, 60, 67-8; Argyle Rink, Boston, 57; Casino Rink, Chicago, 20; Chutes Rink, California, 107; Coliseum Rink, Chicago, 80; Convention Hall Rink, Washington, D.C., 60; Cresent Rink, St. Louis, 60; Delmar Gardens, St. Louis, 60; Denmark Rink, London, 73; Dreamland Rink, Chicago, 62; Earl's Court Rink, London, 60; Elm Rink, New Bedford, MA, 79; Empire Rollerdrome, 109; Grand Hall Olympia, 11; New Dreamland Rink, Newark, 35, 48, 66-7; North Division Street Rink, MI, 80; Oaks Rink, Portland, OR, 90, 106; Olympia Rink, London, 58-9; Palace Rink, Detroit, 61; Palladium, St. Louis, 60, 67; Park City Rink, Brooklyn, 62; Plimpton Skate Rink, 57; Redondo Rink, Redondo, WA, 108; Riverview Rink, Milwaukee, 60-1; Rolladium, Waterford, MI, 104; Rollercade Rink, Cleveland, 81; Rollerdome, Frankfurt, 11; Rollerdome, 67; San Soucci, St. Louis, 60; Select Rink, Augusta, ME, 79; Skating Palace, Paris, 11; Wayne Rink, Detroit, 59; White City Rink, Boise, 64
roller derby, 66-67
Roller Skating Rink Operators Association (RSROA), 22, 34-6, 40-3, 46, 60, 75-6, 81
Roller Skating Spectacular Show, 82

Samual Winslow Roller Skate Company, 19, 34
skates: Allred, 49; Brix, 22; Chicago, 19; Cingar, 9-10; Douglass-Snyder, 49; first recorded use of, 7; Henley, 19, 74; in-line, 9-10, 37, 70-1; parlour, 22; Patin-A-Terre, 8; Petitbled, 8; Plimpton, 13-14, 23; Polar, 20;

"Prophete," 10; Saladee, 22; "Vineyard" model, 19, 27; Volito, 8; Winslow, 19-20, 27; Woodward, 11

skating acts: Artistry on Wheels, 94; Harley Davidson Professional Skating Toupe 59, 61; Helen Carlos Trio, 79; Rexford Troupe, 80; Rexos, The, 79; Skating Vanities, 49, 81-2; Two Kays, 78

Snyder Company, 23

speed, 20-1, 31, 37, 63, 66, 68-71

United States Amateur Confederation of Roller Skating (USAC/RS), (formerly the RSROA), 23, 37, 62, 76-7, 86-7

United States National Amateur Roller Skating Association (USARSA), 36-7

United States Olympic Committee (USOC), 37

USA Roller Skating (formerly the USAC/RS), 37, 86-7

Vanguard Company, 21

vaudeville, 79, 81

Waltz, 15, 25, 39-40, 89-90: Chase Waltz, 40; Continental Waltz, 39

wheels: aluminum alloy, 21; 8 Red Wheels of Canada, 21; Fomac, 21; Hugger, 21; Hyper, 21; ivory, 8; Metaflex, 21; metal, 8; plastic, 21; rubber, 11, 21; steel, 21; Sure-Grip, 21; Tiger Claws, 21; urethane, 21; wood, 7, 8, 19, 21

Wurlitzer organ, 90

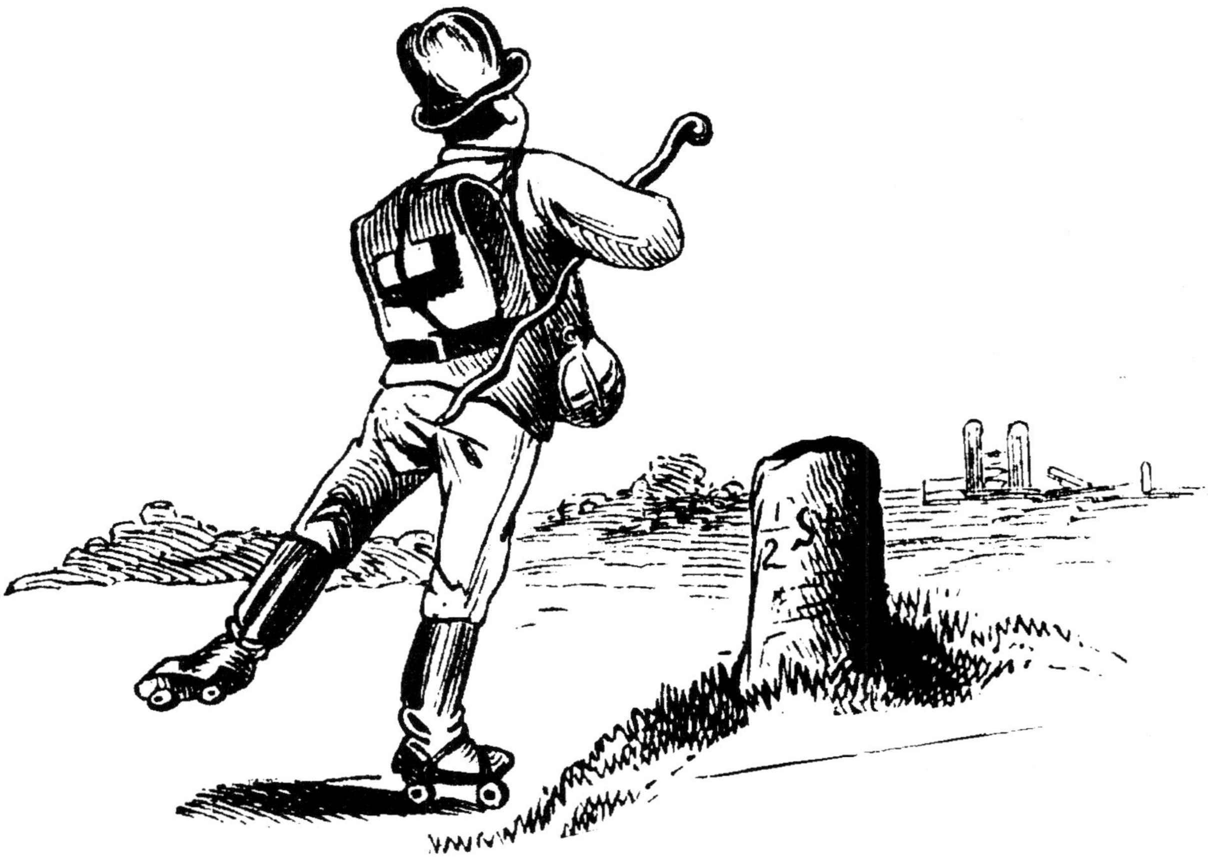